NO GOODBYES

NO GOODBYES

Life-Changing Insights

from the Other Side

BARRY EATON

Jeremy P. Tarcher/Penguin, an imprint of Penguin Random House, *New York*

JEREMY P. TARCHER/PENGUIN
An imprint of Penguin Random House LLC
375 Hudson Street
New York, New York 10014

First published in Australia by Allen & Unwin in 2014
First Tarcher/Penguin paperback edition published in 2015
Copyright © Barry Eaton 2014

Most Tarcher/Penguin books are available at special quantity discounts for bulk purchase for sales promotions, premiums, fund-raising, and educational needs. Special books or book excerpts also can be created to fit specific needs. For details, write: SpecialMarkets@penguinrandomhouse.com.

Library of Congress Cataloging-in-Publication Data

Eaton, Barry.
No goodbyes : life-changing insights from the other side / Barry Eaton.
p.   cm.
Includes bibliographical references.
ISBN 978-0-399-17265-6 (paperback)
1. Death—Psychological aspects.   2. Future life.   3. Bereavement.   4. Mind and body.   I. Title.
BF789.D4E238   2015
133.901'3—dc23
2015005074

Printed in the United States of America
1 3 5 7 9 10 8 6 4 2

Book design by Alissa Theodor

ACKNOWLEDGMENTS

No Goodbyes is dedicated to my late partner, Judy, who now enjoys life in the Heaven World.

My heartfelt thanks go to Kelly and Kristin Dale from the Australian Casa for their love and support.

In the Heaven World, thanks to my guides M, and also John Dingwall and his spiritual team, who have provided so much inspired information. I would be lost without them.

My eternal gratitude to Val Hood, Ezio De Angelis, and Ruth Phillips, three wonderful mediums who have put me in direct contact with the spirit of Judy.

I would like to thank my wonderful mentor and friend Maggie Hamilton, who is always there for me when I ring her for advice or a chat.

Much love to my partner, Anne, for her love and support and also for the valuable editing suggestions she gave me.

Thanks also to Claire Kingston, Mark Lewis, Karen Ward, Angela Handley, and the team at Allen & Unwin for their support.

CONTENTS

Part Two ≈ The Mists of Time

Part Three ≈ New Directions

Part Four ∽ Judy

Part Five ∽ More from the Afterlife Team

INTRODUCTION

———————— ∽ ————————

When you have solved all the mysteries of life you long for
death, for it is but another mystery of life.

—KAHLIL GIBRAN, 1883–1931

One of the great mysteries of life for most people is what will happen to us when we die. Do we just disappear into a black void, never to be seen or heard from again, or is there an afterlife?

Throughout history religions have held out the promise of heavenly rewards to obedient followers who earned the keys to paradise. For others who did not adhere to the rules, the road ahead was full of eternal suffering and pain as punishment for their sins. Sadly, many people still have these beliefs today.

Fear and uncertainty surrounding death prompted me to explore the mysteries of our final journey. As a broadcaster and journalist researching program material, I found my interest piqued by spiritual and metaphysical subjects, prompting the study of astrology in 1991. The uncovering of my psychic abilities soon followed, taking me down many fascinating paths. I conducted a spiritual development group for ten years, connecting with spirit guides and also doing readings.

In 1993 I met Judy, who helped me change my life. Her sudden death only four years later, though devastating, was the catalyst for my latent abilities as a medium to emerge. Judy, now residing in the world of spirit, has inspired and encouraged me to explore and write about the afterlife. Accepting the logical concepts of life after death and reincarnation, I was happy to oblige.

My metaphysics studies have proved to me the power of intention, paramount in any human endeavor. Once I'd committed to writing my first book, *Afterlife*, unexpected opportunities arose, astounding me with their scope, amazing me with insights, and bringing spirits and new people to my life-affirming quest.

When I opened my heart and mind to write, I was honored and excited to connect to the bountiful, loving, and inspiring energy of a new guide, simply called M. More about my relationship with this highly advanced master spirit will be explored and revealed later.

The afterlife—or as Judy appealingly called it, "the Heaven World," when she spoke to me through the medium Ezio De Angelis—is invisible to us on earth. It exists in what is essentially another dimension.

After reading *Afterlife*, many people contacted me to say how they had been inspired to make positive changes to their lives. Others said how grateful they were to be able to release the fear of death that they had previously felt. Once we accept the fact that we do reunite with our loved ones when we pass over, we can take another load off our minds. When we accept that the soul is indestructible and life is eternal, we realize there is no such thing as "death." We can let go of our fears and truly live each day to the fullest. Judy and I have shared many past lives, and will see each other again when I, too, return home to the Heaven World.

We may regard the earthly civilization we have created as complex, but it is just a tiny reflection of the vast size and scope of the spirit world. As my contact with those in the spirit world continued, I soon discovered that *Afterlife* had only scratched the surface.

No Goodbyes now takes us much deeper into this fascinating world.

Part One

Going Deeper

1

Where to Explore Next?

My partner Judy died in 1997 after a brief illness. We had been together for four intense and tumultuous years, which were fortunately also full of fun, loving, and laughter.

Judy's sudden passing shattered me for a long time. I had finally been reunited with my soul mate, only to lose her again so quickly. But a few months later we reconnected, as her spirit reassuringly spoke to me across the divide from the afterlife, via the medium Ruth Phillips. This connection with Judy was the beginning of a whole new life for both of us. As with most deaths, there is a hidden gift as well as the grief we experience when our loved one departs. When we are emotionally ready, we just have to look for this gift, which is not always an easy task, as it may not be obvious. My gift from Judy was the realization of my abilities as a medium, a process that has unfolded over the intervening years and continues to this day.

We have stayed in touch ever since. In a way Judy has become my spiritual muse. At first she was what I termed my "spirit wrangler," as she gathered together other spirits in the afterlife for one-on-one readings and for the group development work that I was conducting.

An amazing series of events then unfolded. As the new millennium opened, I had "graduated" from working solely in mainstream broadcasting and journalism to produce and host an Internet radio show, *Radio Out There*, which covers all aspects of mind, body, and spirit themes. In many ways this proved to be the backbone for *Afterlife*, as I have been fortunate enough to interview hundreds of people from all over the world, many of whom specialize in life after death.

There is really no such thing as death. We are all eternal spiritual energies attaching ourselves to a physical body in order to have a human experience. We enjoy many lives, and our basic purpose is to have a full range of experiences so that we can grow and develop. We all return to the same place, a vast Heaven World, which is often referred to as the afterlife, comprising many levels and planes of existence, which surrounds our earthly world.

The Heaven World vibrates at a much faster rate than does the dense energy of the earth. This world is invisible to us on earth, existing in what is essentially another dimension, and is our real home. We leave it only to reincarnate and have a multitude of experiences by attaching our spirit to a physical body on earth, and also on other worlds.

Every contact I have had with spirits in the afterlife reinforces the fact that there is no such place as hell. However, adhering to the principle of "As above, so below," there are lower levels where some dark spirits find themselves after leading violent, toxic, or degenerate lives. But forget any images of demons in a fiery pit armed with nasty pitchforks and evil grins—here the dark spirits are helped in a loving way by advanced spirits. Any "punishment" suffered is self-inflicted by the spirit once they look back in a life review with a Council of Elders on their previous activities. No matter what they have done, these dark spirits are given loving assistance to grow and develop before returning for another life.

When we return to the afterlife after each incarnation, we automatically find ourselves at the appropriate level of our soul development. We are able to communicate here only with the power of thought, as of course not having a body means no vocal cords. We communicate and create the environment in which we live through our thoughts.

The Heaven World is a place of love, peace, and spiritual support, helping us understand and embrace our full power as individual souls. The way we live our lives on earth directly affects our life and position in the world of spirit when we return after each sojourn. There is an old saying, "You can't take it with you when you go," but I beg to differ. Yes, we do leave our material things behind when we transition to the afterlife—they are of no use there—but what we do take with us is the spiritual legacy of the life we have just lived.

As an astrologer, psychic, and Johnny-come-lately medium, I was able to delve deeply into this fascinating world. Fueled by a curiosity to know as much as I could about life after death, I underwent some intense past-life regression. One notable exploration took me back to my last incarnation as Brian, a young British soldier who died in the bloody Battle of the Somme in July 1916. Remarkably, Brian took me on a huge voyage of rediscovery as I experienced his return to the world of spirit after his painful death in World War I.

When we return to the afterlife, every spirit passes through a healing center to release any residual effects of that past lifetime. Looking on from the sidelines, I followed Brian as he went into the healing center to cleanse his spirit after his grueling wartime experiences, afterward meeting the Council of Elders for his life review. There are many such councils comprising advanced loving spirits who oversee our spiritual progression. Finally he reconnected with his soul family in the afterlife to begin a period of rest, revision, and eventual preparation for his next life. Along the way Brian revealed to me how people live in the afterlife, their work, how they interact with their guides and other spirits, and also how they relax and enjoy their spiritual respite.

The wonderful thing about connecting with those who have passed over into the afterlife is that nothing can be taken for granted. Just when I thought I had all the answers I needed about the world of spirit, the powers that be decided to bring me back to earth with a thud.

When *Afterlife* was published, my natural thought process was to wonder . . . what next? Despite the fact that nothing immediately leaped into my mind as I cogitated and put out for guidance, Spirit obviously had it all mapped out.[1]

I was still communicating with the spirit of former screenwriter and film producer John Dingwall via the trance mediumship of his son, Kelly Dale. John had contributed a lot of fine detail to my earlier research on the spirit world documented in *Afterlife*, and Kelly wanted to keep channeling his father for personal reasons. We both felt this ongoing contact would also help Kelly as he developed his considerable talents in this area.

Kelly is a natural trance medium, and I have been working with him for many years, assisting him to use his skills in connecting with Spirit. Trance mediums allow spirits to communicate by using the their physical body while they are in deep trance, unlike those who communicate with spirits while fully conscious. He's now able to reach deep within himself to a place of peace and security, one where he is happy to rest quietly and allow an appropriate spiritual contact to share his body. Sometimes he remembers at the end of the session who has come through, but details are always sketchy at best. He refuses to listen back to our recorded sessions, to honor the integrity of the information received. He later became familiar with details of his father's life in spirit after reading *Afterlife*.

Once *Afterlife* was published, I moved to a very peaceful area close to the Australian Casa, a branch of John of God's healing center in Brazil. Situated on Kelly's property, Eagles Nest, the casa is on an elevated ridge with sweeping views to the ocean, and the energy there is strong and pure. The calm and luxuriant natural environment is very conducive to quiet reflection and meditation, and we decided that whenever time permitted, Kelly would come to my house. He wanted to continue our sessions, as he felt a strong emotional bond with his father in the afterlife, and wished to maintain it. In our first session I thanked John Dingwall and his spirit friends for their contribution to the book, presuming that I had gone as far as we could go on the subject of the afterlife, and was just there for a chat. However, with John's response, I was smartly pulled into line. He told me my book was just the beginning! There was a lot more information from Spirit that needed to be put into at least one more book.

To say I was taken aback is quite an understatement. I sat there with my mouth agape, for once in my life almost speechless. John went on to say that the advanced spirits in the afterlife are in the process of a concerted information drive to help people worldwide release their fears about death and embrace the fact that life is a continuing process. They also believe the time is right for people to be given as much information as possible about the continuing thread of eternal life, by revealing detailed facts about life in the world of spirit. John was selected as just one of many spirit communicators to work with people on the earth plane in every possible way to get the message out.

Subsequent research shows that Spirit was very active in this regard from the late nineteenth century through to the 1920s, a few years after the end of the Great War. In those years, there was a huge interest in the afterlife, because of various factors, including the huge loss of life in the war. Unfortunately this interest faded with the pursuit of scientific subjects taking over from the spiritual.

However, things are changing again, as people are asking questions that remain unanswered by science and other belief systems. We are constantly being sent messages from many different sources in spirit, embracing everything from more widespread contact with loved ones in the afterlife to the much-publicized subject of raising consciousness to new levels of awareness. The ongoing flow of information about our relationship with the world of spirit is an important part of our personal growth as well as that of society as a whole. Most important, with the increasing sophistication of communications technology, more and more people are starting to seek out this information.

Well, that certainly answered the question of what to write for the next book.

It was also the beginning of a series of communications with John Dingwall acting as the "spokespirit" for a specially selected group of spirits whose combined wisdom was channeled through his son, Kelly. There is nothing new in this procedure, as spirits communicating with mediums at séances conducted a century ago always referred to a "spirit control" as their inspiration. Whether mediums work in their conscious mind in a trance, they still work through a spirit control.

As our sessions unfolded over many months, John took us deeper and deeper into his world, revealing more aspects of the afterlife and exploring some of the mysteries of life itself. I soon discovered the truth of the saying "As above, so below."

After a few sessions we decided the energy was more powerful for Kelly to do the sessions in a healing room adjoining the Australian

Casa. Our spirit connection was immediately enhanced and became stronger as the weeks progressed. Kelly's wife, Kristin, joined us in each session, as she and I needed to generate as much energy as possible to help John and Kelly maintain the levels needed for clear communication during the trance mediumship. Kristin usually conducts the regular meditation meetings at the Australian Casa and has become a strong channel. In the higher vibration of the afterlife, many spirits are needed to focus the energy levels required for trance sessions of this nature.

With Kristin's strong support we were able to delve more deeply into the world of spirit than I had in the past. I was also inspired by the collective energy of a team of spirits to ask questions on subjects that I had not previously even thought of, obtaining fascinating extra layers of information about our ongoing life in spirit. Often these questions suddenly "popped" into my head, taking us into exciting new areas of exploration. I have since become convinced that this is part of the communication by thought that is available to us all when we are able to clear our mind of the barriers and distractions of our fast-paced daily lives and open ourselves to the possibility of spirit contact. As no voice boxes are available to spirits, most communication is done through thought transmission and physical sensations, unless they can speak through a trance medium. Some mediums use instruments to help spirits speak in séances, and a voice box device was very popular in Victorian times and is sometimes still used today.

My partner Judy transitioned to the afterlife in 1997, leaving me the gift of the opening to mediumship. When we are able to come to terms with the grief of people very close to us passing over, we will inevitably discover they have left us a spiritual gift. It may be self-awareness, forgiveness, freedom, realization of unconditional love, or one of countless other benefits that we were not aware of previously. With John giving fresh instructions to assist with a more in-depth afterlife exploration, I determined to find out as much as I could about Judy's new life. A serendipitous meeting with UK medium Val Hood provided the catalyst for this exciting new series of contacts with Judy in the world of spirit. My good friend Ezio De Angelis made a further connection with Judy some months later. These wonderful communications proved to be a very important part of my research, and will be covered in detail in later chapters.

Most of us have had many past lives. Who and where we are in this lifetime is the karmic culmination point for all of our experiences so far. However, with the large population on earth now, new souls are constantly arriving here as well. Those people who have been around the traps many times are often referred to as "old souls." New or old, we can all learn a lot about ourselves by exploring our past, as I was able to do after discovering my incarnation as Brian. The journey that his spirit made through the Heaven World, described in detail in *Afterlife*, whetted my appetite for more revelations, so I decided to delve further into the mists of time to explore more of my past. I received several shocks, which have provided fascinating material for many chapters later in this book.

One afternoon, during this period of past-life research, I was in deep meditation at the Australian Casa when I received a very strong message from Spirit: "The seeds of each life contain our past, and our lessons can be disguised as pain."

My guide, simply known as M, later confirmed that this thought was given to me by Judy's spirit, who I have been told is around me a lot of the time, along with M, especially while I am researching and writing about the afterlife.

The message resonated strongly at the time and stayed with me for several weeks, but as I dived deeper and deeper into the whirlpool of my own past I came to realize the truth of this revelation.

Once you realize that the road is the goal and that you
are always on the road, not to reach a goal, but to enjoy its
beauty and its wisdom, life ceases to be a task and becomes
natural and simple, in itself an ecstasy.

—SRI NISARGADATTA MAHARAJ, 1897–1981,
philosopher and spiritual teacher

2

Voices from Above

At first it was difficult to establish regular connections with John and the spirit group. Kelly is not a full-time medium. He attends to the upkeep of his property as well as running the Australian Casa and is also a devoted family man with many demands on his time and energy. Taking a couple of hours out of his day to go into trance was not always easy, and Kelly also had to be in the right spiritual energy for it to work. Trance mediumship can also be physically draining, so we had to plan our sessions carefully.

As the sessions with John's group progressed, the energy needed for clear communication between our two worlds intensified. John told us that a spirit cannot just decide to connect through a trance medium; support energy from other spirits is needed.

We quickly realized that John had not suddenly become the font of all knowledge, but was part of a combined and highly organized effort to impart information. John told us that advanced spirit helpers and teachers were working with him in each session to generate the energy required for our communications, as well as providing a reference source. As our sessions progressed John was soon able to virtually channel instant information from these higher sources as well as give us his own personal observations. If he didn't know the answer to a question he would ask more advanced spirits in his support group, or for the more complex questions he was able to go away and gather information for our next session.

John described himself as a facilitator or host for his particular energy group. Often he did not know what was going to be said or relayed in our sessions; he said that sometimes it felt almost as if the information flow had been taken out of his hands. Because communication in the afterlife is purely by thought, with John as our host we were able to tune in to the thoughts of the whole group. My guide M later confirmed that the group energy we are communicating with comprises many advanced spirits at various levels in the afterlife. According to M, John is apparently also advancing rapidly in his own soul development, which is why he was chosen to host this group.

Just as we have a hierarchy on earth, so are there many levels or planes of existence in the afterlife. Advancement for each person to higher planes is determined by the growth of his or her soul over many lifetimes. This differs from the skills, contacts, and corporate and political means that we need to employ to progress in our daily lives on earth.

The highly evolved spirits working with the group are not actually congregating in the same place, but can send their energy and their thoughts to the main group from wherever they are located. They are able to fragment their energy, so that they can be working with John as part of the information flow while still carrying out many other activities at the same time.

> *Believe there is a great power silently working all things for good, behave yourself, and never mind the rest.*
>
> —BEATRIX POTTER, 1866–1943,
> author and illustrator

My spirit guide, M, who is a highly advanced spirit, is once again by my side, and every now and then my fingers on the keyboard respond unconsciously to his thoughts and directions. As I write about John and his group, M reminds me of my former work as a newsreader, for the purpose of comparison. While the audience sees or hears someone reading the news, the broadcaster is really only the front person for a whole team of people who have prepared the bulletin to go to air. Reporters, journalists, and producers, all backed by a support staff and headed by management, combine to bring the message to the audience. Their individual experience and skills are needed to ensure a successful team effort.

M tells me that it is a similar situation with John's messages, and like the multitude of radio and TV stations broadcasting regular news bulletins in countries all over the world, ours is one of many such groups broadcasting from the afterlife. However, the intrinsic message is universal: Life continues beyond death, and soul evolution achieved through a multitude of experiences is the main reason we undergo life in a physical body.

One of the questions that puzzles many people is the difference between the soul and the spirit. It was important for John's team to answer this question at the start of our new quest.

Essentially they are two separate energies that combine as one. The soul is the indestructible and perfect essence, which originally emerges from the Creator Spirit, or the Source, and embarks on a series of earthly adventures to explore and learn as much as possible until it eventually has no further need of a physical body. The spirit is the vehicle that the soul uses to have these experiences, both on earth and in the afterlife.

The soul, utilizing the energy of the spirit, attaches itself to the heart of our physical body so that it can have as many human experiences as possible in each lifetime. After each lifetime the soul returns to the afterlife to rest, reflect, and prepare for the next adventure. As John pointed out, that is why everything begins and ends with the heart. The two words *heart* and *soul* are often linked in our everyday conversations, such as "embracing something with all your heart and soul"; there have been countless popular songs, also a few films, with that title; many businesses also are registered under that name. At some level it appears we are happy to believe that the heart and soul are one.

Once we can accept that the soul is indestructible and life is eternal, we realize there is no such thing as "death." We can release our fears and truly live each day to the fullest.

3

Crossing Over into a New Life

Perhaps it is my curiosity as someone who loves interviewing people that has led me down the track of investigating the afterlife. All I can say is that the more information I am given about the world of spirit and our relationship to it, the more questions spring up in my mind.

Feeling a little like Lewis Carroll's famous literary character Alice, I invite you to join me as we further explore this timeless wonderland that we are all part of, and to which we will all return—again and again. So without further ado let us go behind the looking glass of our earthly life on an exciting voyage of discovery.

One of my favorite activities is people watching. Sitting in an outdoor café, sipping a coffee and watching the passing parade is a fascinating way to spend some time. As each face drifts or rushes by, absorbed in its own reality, it is intriguing how many unique stories are being played out all over the world every day. Every person is the star of his or her own personal drama.

Each of us experiences the end of life in a unique way. Some people are well prepared and ready to make the return journey home when the time comes, happy to reconnect with friends and family in spirit. Others cross over in great fear and denial. Some have no expectations of an afterlife, and spend the first part of their new journey coming to terms with the fact that life actually continues. These deceased people usually spend a period of adjustment in a sphere of reality they have created for themselves. This can often be a gray, misty world or even a place of complete darkness, sometimes referred to as the "shadow lands."

The one thing we all have in common is that we eventually return to the world of spirit, no matter what our earthly status.

Once the game is over, the king and the pawn go back into
the same box.

—ITALIAN PROVERB

The experiences we have in the afterlife, along with the contacts we make and the way we view our new conditions, depend on the individual spirit. It is no different from the way we lead our earthly lives, in which our environment, education, and the people around us, together with the choices and decisions we make, combine to create our reality. Each one of us represents the sum total of all our past experiences, and our actions and reactions reflect this history. We also live and work mainly in groups of people, family, friends, and colleagues, each of whom has a widely differing outlook on life as well as their own diverse activities and behavior patterns.

So it would be naive to think that we would all have the same experiences in leaving our body and crossing over into the world of spirit. It is perhaps similar to visiting another country on earth; each person has a unique experience with the people and events encountered, and shapes them accordingly. At the end of their travels, all people return home with their own special memories and photographs.

Our beliefs and activities in each life will determine the direction we take when we return to the spirit world. Those people who accept their ongoing existence, or who at least cross over with an open mind, are able to make the transition to the afterlife easily. When factors such as fear, ignorance, skepticism, and fundamentalism come into play, they can create blockages that need to be dealt with before that spirit can advance.

Ignorance is a big factor, especially in the event of a sudden passing. John spoke of children, teenagers, and others who had not thought about what happens after death. Because of that ignorance they often cross over in a state of confusion, but are then met by loving spirits who explain their new situation to them. This new existence must come as a shock to the skeptics who thought they were about to disappear into the world of eternal darkness. It seems to me that families need to talk to their children about all aspects of life, instead of leaving it to others, or letting them find out for themselves the hard way. This includes the transitional process that we call death.

John also spoke of those who cross over with ingrained archetypal beliefs of heaven and hell. When there are no Pearly Gates, no Saint Peter welcoming them, no traditional images of angels fluttering about in the sky, not even a harp on the horizon; quite often they believe they have arrived in hell. They can form a false impression because of the fundamental beliefs that have been programmed into their minds.

Sometimes in these confusing situations guilt comes into play, and then fear may take over, making their arrival in the afterlife very challenging for them and also for their family and friends waiting for them there. For a time many of these people live in denial and fear, according to John, who also works as part of a welcoming group for newcomers as one of his many duties in spirit. He revealed that it can be very difficult to help these new arrivals emerge from their set frame of mind and adjust to what is really happening around them.

John also pointed out that sometimes even evolved souls may have problems adjusting to the spirit world again, as they have left behind loved ones and find their last life very difficult to release. However, when they realize they can still make contact with those on earth, a huge weight is lifted from them. They know they have to leave the earth plane behind, but when they discover that they can still be in a position to eventually guide and help their loved ones, it is a lot easier.

Apparently, though, not all spirits want to stay in close contact with those on the earth plane; some are more than happy to let go of everything and everyone from that past life. They adopt the principle of "been there, done that" and are ready to move on. Contact is an individual choice, but sometimes it may be part of a soul's destiny to immediately move on, as it is possible to return to higher planes to evolve or perhaps even to teach others in the afterlife. This allows them to release their earthly ties more easily, and also explains why some people communicate with loved ones back on earth, while others are never heard from again.

Just as on earth, everybody in the afterlife has tasks to carry out, and once settled in, is keen to pursue a range of new activities. Many people opt to continue with the activities they enjoyed in their previous life, and these can range from practical pursuits to artistic and cultural interests. Others prefer to pursue completely different activities, perhaps learning new skills or indulging in creative areas such as painting, music, or acting, which they were unable to enjoy in their previous life. Yes, they do produce plays and even films there!

John has continued to write in the afterlife, but chuckled as he told us he does not have to use his old typewriter, saying, "It's a lot simpler now, as essentially information is gathered and then passed on."

Spirits are also allotted other duties, which can range from assisting new arrivals to assimilate through to helping in one of the healing centers or places of learning. The level of this work depends on the soul's development.

As on earth we can choose our leisure activities, so in the afterlife can we explore pursuits that may be creative, sporting, or whatever. John gave the example of a fisherman who still goes fishing every day, not just to catch fish, but to be part of and embrace the natural sights and sounds of his surroundings. The fisherman can enjoy the experience, even without a physical body. John described this as more of a sensation, such as we may experience in a vivid dream. Maybe my golf swing will improve when I get back there.

John said he still chooses to retain a sense of sight, even though he has no physical eyes to see through. He likens it to seeing a picture in the mind's eye, which is the way a clairvoyant sees images. This method of vision apparently forms a crystal-clear picture in the mind's eye of each spirit. Memory also plays a part in conjuring up these images for him. This is how he is able to play sports, watch films, and take part in any number of activities.

In the afterlife we are able to create these conditions and feelings with our thoughts, and John believes that in many ways they are a lot stronger and better than what we can experience with our physical bodies. However, while the fisherman may catch and even eat the fish he has created and then caught, this is unnecessary, as food and drink are not needed for a spirit body. Still, old habits die hard.

When people first arrive back in the afterlife they usually sit down and have meals, make cups of tea and coffee, smoke, and even enjoy an alcoholic beverage. They are able to create these experiences through the power of thought and memory. The feeling and habits of the human body—even though they're now in spirit form—are often so strong and ingrained that the need to eat and drink and indulge in other earthly activities stays with us until we are ready to release it.

John reminisced about his craving for chocolate for desserts when he first crossed over, and said this indulgence took a while to fade. However, he added that his choices still include occasionally indulging in food and drink, even though he has no physical body to sustain. These are cravings of the mind, as opposed to actual needs, and remain with many spirits in the afterlife until they eventually fade. The same applies to habits such as drinking alcohol and smoking, especially if the people concerned have had deep conditioning in the previous life.

John went on to introduce the topic of addictive drugs, which he described as having the biggest influence on the soul's pathway. They are generally the saddest souls in the afterlife as they struggle with their addiction, which has totally affected the purpose of their previous life. Drug use leaves an imprint on the psyche that is difficult to remove. Sometimes this imprint even remains ingrained as those spirits move into their next incarnation, as part of their karma, so that they can continue to learn lessons about their addictions.

As I explained in *Afterlife*, any therapy needed around addictions begins in the healing center, where the spirit is sent shortly after crossing over. However, healing some addictions can be a very complex process with long-term effects that require a lot of subsequent soul group work and counseling.

Situations like these are closely examined by spirits in afterlife group sessions with their guides as part of each soul's learning process. They are able to ascertain how this dependence impacted on them and others in their last life, and also investigate the reason for their addiction. In some instances addiction could be related to the experiences that people in their family or social circle needed to have.

This linking thread between us all is a very complex story, and John will explain it in a later chapter. The team also had a lot to say in future sessions on the topic of addiction to drugs. It expressed concern about the growing use of illegal and recreational drugs and the imprint they can make on the spirit of the people using them. Inappropriate or excessive use of some medications also can have an apparent impact on the spirit. Once a spirit returns to the afterlife, these imprints need cleansing, which can be an arduous process.

4

The Puzzling Question of Time

Before each session with Kelly and John, I would meditate on what topics to discuss. M often chimed in with his suggestions, and I would sometimes wake up with an exciting new direction to pursue. John usually seemed to know what I wanted to discuss when we connected and would sometimes preempt my questions. At other times, questions would be fed into my mind as the session progressed, and often opened up exciting new areas of discussion.

One such topic reemerged at our next session.

We had discussed in one of our very early communications that there is no such thing as time in the world of spirit; there is only the present moment to be experienced. Time is purely a measurement humans have created by using earth's annual 365-day journey around the sun to give themselves some kind of reference in their daily lives. But if we lived on Mercury, which takes only 88 days to orbit the sun, this formula would be completely different, so time is subjective.

People have always been fascinated by the measurement of time, with the oldest records being found in India, where measurement started by relating elapsed time to the blinking of the eye. It was found that this averaged at four seconds' duration and was called a *paramanu*. In an alternate system described in the Vishnu Purana book, it is stated that fifteen twinklings of the eye equaled one *káshtihá*. Fortunately for us, the sun system turned out to be more popular, although some people still describe events as happening "in the blink of an eye."

The whole question of time fascinates me, probably because of my career in radio and TV, in which things are usually precisely measured in seconds. When I worked as a newsreader or program presenter, being exactly on time was vital. It's no use turning up a couple of minutes after the program goes to air; the silence would be deafening. But in spirit it's a different story.

When I was communicating with the spirit world many years ago, time was explained to me as like a giant circle that loops back on itself. Perhaps it would help to explain the concept that past, present, and future are all happening simultaneously, and not on a linear path, and allows us to experience many lives at the same time. It also brings into play the concept of parallel dimensions. My brain finds this very hard to absorb, but Sid Caesar, a US actor, writer, and comedian, summed it up brilliantly:

There's a now, a was, and a gonna be. Now is now, and after now is a was. And what comes after the was is a gonna be. It hasn't happened yet. It's gonna happen as soon as the now is over. But if you have a good now, you're bound to have a good was and a good gonna be.

But after the bad now comes a bad was. But if you have a bad now and dwell on it, you're going to have a bad gonna be and you're going to have a bad cycle. If you learn from the bad was, you can turn the bad gonna be into a good gonna be. The only way you can change the cycle is after the was. If you carry the bad wases around with you, they get heavy and become should'a could'as—I should'a done this, I could'a done that.

If you learn from the was, you'll have a great now; you won't repeat the same mistakes. It will bring you to a good now, which changes the cycle to a good was, and a good gonna be. You need to learn from the wases. It's all about changing your attitude.[1]

Not a bad formula for life, really.

One of the first questions I asked John Dingwall once we got back into contact was how spirits in the afterlife know when an event like a concert or a lecture is about to start, if there is no point of reference.

His answer made me think a lot. He said people have to create their own reality in the spirit world, using the power of thought for any scheduled event to take place. He likened it to direct streaming through the Internet, or even the concept of delayed broadcasts. I immediately understood his meaning, as my radio program, *Radio*

Out There, is prerecorded and streamed onto the Internet and can be accessed whenever listeners choose to visit my Web site, wherever they are in the world. John had a smile in his voice when he said that on earth we are gradually catching up with the "technology" used in the afterlife. I wonder how he could have explained that before the digital age.

We are observed by those in the world of spirit as trapping ourselves as slaves to time in our earthly lives, from the moment we open our eyes each morning, probably to the sound of an alarm clock for most people. The constraints around time are a very difficult cycle to break, I am told. When he first returned to his home in the afterlife, John found it difficult to adjust to the complete absence of time, and he admits he is still working on this, even after being there for several earth years. He described his mind as still being "humanish," which means he rises at the same "time" and feels he has to meet someone at a set "time." However, in the afterlife there is only the state of the present moment, or being "in the now," as it is often referred to these days. In fact, John does not have to sleep—it's not needed in the afterlife—but sometimes chooses to do so out of habit.

A guest on my radio program provided an insight into the question of time. Jim Self, a spiritual teacher from the United States, maintains that people on earth now live between two dimensions. The third dimension is one of linear measurement in which we gauge things in a straight line, such as past, present, and future. However, Jim believes that part of our spiritual energy is moving into the fourth dimension, where there is no such thing as time, only the present moment. Humans find it very difficult to escape the restrictions imposed by a linear world, and must make a conscious effort to be in the moment. When we stop and tune in to our thoughts, we are mostly thinking about either past or future events. It requires a conscious decision for us to focus on the present moment.

This becomes evident when we watch someone on TV playing competitive sports. Commentators will refer to the way a player is focusing on the moment, but when mistakes are made, they often comment that it is because the player has lost concentration.

Because the afterlife is located in a higher dimension than that of the earth and time does not exist there, spirits have to revert to three-dimensional thinking to be able to plan their contacts with us.

On a slightly different vein, the thought came to me as the session progressed to inquire about the weather in the world of spirit. I have never seen or heard any references to rain, wind, or storms in the Heaven World, so apparently they experience what might be thought of as perfect weather conditions. Many people in the afterlife do speak of being bathed in a warm, constant light, but do not report seeing the sun as such, although John still chooses to experience the energy of the sun. It would seem to me that once the sun cycle is taken out of the equation in that dimension, time measurement has no basis or reason for existence.

It seems that while three-dimensional thinking is available on certain levels of the afterlife, not all spirits choose to use it; some choose to live there in "a different manner." Some advanced spirits choose to exist "almost like thin air, feeling their way through life," according to John. They exist on higher levels, but move around as part of their work as teachers and guides. Everyone has a choice in how they wish to live, and this is their preference.

As spirits advance to higher levels they are able to split their energy and be in many places at once. They are able to achieve this as part of the escape from linear time in a world where past, present, and future actually happen simultaneously, a principle difficult for the human mind to grasp. John gave the example of looking at a star shining brightly in the night sky: even though we can see the star's light we know that the star isn't actually shining at that moment but is a number of light-years away, or perhaps the star died a long time ago; however, it exists for us in the past, present, and future.

The advanced spirits want us to know that until we can learn to get over our dependence on time, we will not be able to access other dimensions of reality, despite our having the inherent ability to do so.

Look well to this day. Yesterday is but a dream and
tomorrow is only a vision. But today well lived makes every
yesterday a dream of happiness and every tomorrow a
vision of hope. Look well therefore to this day.

—EXCERPT FROM AN ANCIENT SANSKRIT POEM

5

Destiny and Free Will

The question of destiny versus free will is one that has vexed many people over the ages. I have always maintained that life as a human being on earth combines both of these principles, and it is up to us to define the difference. After all, if every aspect of our lives was predestined, what would be the point of it all? We would merely be marionettes manipulated by some celestial puppeteer as part of a script over which we have no input. And, according to my guide M, if everything was purely free will, chaos would reign supreme.

"We all have a destiny, everything and everybody have a purpose." Those words from John were firm and absolute, leaving no room for argument. As a former journalist, John has spent a lot of his afterlife activities researching the question of destiny and free will, as he has always been interested in what makes people tick. He is still on a relentless pursuit for truth, which has always been his watchword.

John has discovered that our destiny plays an important part in our future lives, and said it's a key issue in group discussions in the afterlife as people prepare for their next incarnation. To what extent destiny impacts our lives varies with each person. It could be compared with the plot points in a mystery movie, providing options for new directions, opportunities, and challenges. Free will then takes over as we relate and react to each destiny point. The decisions we make form a vital part of our soul growth, as we learn to take responsibility for our actions. Or not, as the case might be.

Just to confuse the issue, John has now learned that at times we may also have conflicting destinies, requiring us to take responsibility, whether we like it or not. The choices we make at these paradoxical times can affect the whole course of our life. When we then exercise our free will, it makes life really challenging. Temptations placed in our way test our character, or we may also become victims of circumstances. John gave the example of people's destiny being dramatically altered when they decide to take drugs. This may open up a whole new life path, taking them well away from the destiny route they were following at the time. They may be happy to continue in this new direction, even if it proves damaging for themselves and for others. However, there is always the opportunity available to return to their original predestined path. Although John emphasized it is vital that they accept responsibility for their choices and actions.

He added that while temptations may be placed in our way by our guides for our potential growth, there are also "bad spirits out there" who take satisfaction from disrupting and sometimes even ruining people's lives. These are often described as mischievous spirits or dark energies. They are trapped or choose to stay behind on the earth plane after death. Many of them are afraid to cross over because of past deeds, and others will not accept that they are dead.

Many aspects of our destiny come into play, and these can be stretched over numerous lifetimes. Sometimes we fulfill our destiny in one lifetime, but there are too many potential scenarios to generalize. We all have specific destiny points where we connect with key people such as family, friends, colleagues, even adversaries. We can also agree to meet up with certain people from past lifetimes to complete our karma with them, or to continue long-cherished relationships. This may involve members of our immediate soul group, but not always.

Certain aspects of our life are meant to be, whether we like it or not. John likens this to the number of veins in a human body. Some are large and obvious, moving on a certain path, with smaller ones hidden or difficult to see, but on close inspection most rejoin the destined route. Some also cross, head off in other directions, and never come back to that point. Your destiny may be found on one of the clearly defined lines, but the distraction caused by smaller diversions could change things completely. Once again, this is where free will comes into play.

John described the activities associated with these veins as forming part of a gigantic tapestry in which we are all featured in some way. Sometimes our threads cross over, linking up with other strands and heading in new directions, but in most cases we spend much of our lives working on our own small patch. There is a popular Chinese legend that maintains there is a red thread coming from each of us that connects us with those we are destined to meet, regardless of time, place, or circumstance. The thread may stretch or tangle, but will never break.

The whole subject of destiny brings up various questions in my mind. I have interviewed many people who achieve prominence in life. Are they playing out a destiny mapped out in their life contract before they reincarnated? Taking it to a different level, what about world events that occur on a grand scale: Are they predestined?

John confirmed my thought that people who have risen to great prominence or had major achievements in their life have fulfilled a prior destiny. He added it also indicates that certain parts of history have been pre-written to some extent, and the key people involved were given a lot of help and guidance along the way.

John's information, which comes from his teachers and advanced spirits, implies that certain influential figures in history, such as Martin Luther King Jr., Nelson Mandela, Winston Churchill, John F. Kennedy, and Abraham Lincoln, are old souls. They are advanced spiritual beings who were capable of handling the pressure on them and were able to make vital decisions when placed in situations of high duress that changed the course of history.

Major events, such as the two world wars of the twentieth century, were predestined to a degree. However, when certain key figures closely involved in these wars allowed their power to corrupt them, the conflicts escalated and spiraled out of control, way past the point that was originally destined.

With regard to the grim figures of history, John pointed out that sometimes evil is born out of evil, but some infamous figures have inspired other people and events that have proved life changing, even beneficial, in the long term. Many dark situations have eventually led to huge positive changes in the world.

The First World War saw huge loss of life, but there were great advancements in technology, including the establishment of air combat as the battles raged on for more than four years. Planes became faster, bigger, and more sophisticated. When peace was declared, there were many trained pilots ready to take up the opportunity as air transport was soon recognized as the way of the future.

I was very surprised to hear John go on to say that the spirit world has an almost impossible task of controlling evil once it escalates, as it is born out of fear and hate. With regard to the world wars, once enmity escalated them into brutal conflicts, nothing could be done to halt their progress. These events created a destiny of their own, which led to world-changing events such as the Depression, mass migration, new European borders formed, and new countries such as Israel created. Would these events have occurred as a matter of course, or did the world wars irrevocably change the destiny of hundreds of millions of people?

The question remains, whether commanders such as Dwight Eisenhower, Field Marshal Bernard Montgomery, and General Douglas MacArthur, who rose to such prominence in the Second World War, would have achieved their place in history without winning major battles.

John reminded me that spirits about to reincarnate can embrace their destiny in many ways to learn their karmic lessons. Rising to prominence is one way, but even leading a simple life helping others can mean fulfilling your destiny in that particular lifetime.

When I asked him whether many great figures in history have reincarnated or are still residing in the afterlife, his reply was: "It's not as if these details are up on a billboard somewhere, but word does get around in the spirit world just like on earth." When an important spirit visits the plane you inhabit, someone invariably knows who it was in a previous life. It is not encouraged but, as John said, people still gossip even in the afterlife.

My guide M wished to speak on the subject of destiny and life contracts, which he describes as such a complicated and vital part of our experiences. Pre-arranged contact between people before incarnation involves many activities and emotions, whether they occur in relationships, the workplace, or on a casual basis. While we may upset someone by causing problems in their life, this may have been arranged in spirit for their ultimate benefit and perhaps ours as well. Later, when our circumstances change, we often realize that life has taken a fresh turn or new opportunities have arisen, and work out for the better. These apparent setbacks may occur because of many events, from emotional outbursts and karma to being fired or retrenched, accidents, illness, and of course broken relationships. However, it is important that we do not use these setbacks as an excuse to indulge in unacceptable behavior, otherwise we are only negatively impacting others' lives while potentially creating bad karma for ourselves.

6

Challenges to Life Paths

So, how can we determine what is predestined or part of our karma? This is a difficult question that arises when we examine the concept of destiny. Are personality traits, such as those found in someone who is a chocoholic or overaggressive or an addicted gambler, predestined or karmic?

According to John, either situation can apply, especially if the personality trait grows and is allowed to result in an extreme problem in later life. Severe disorders can pose enormous challenges. It is ultimately an individual's voluntary choice, a reaction of free will and not divine determination, to overcome them. John cited the example of the effects of one hundred people being injected with heroin.

A percentage of them could go on to become addicts, while others would suffer no ongoing effects.

John went on to say that a destiny path does not necessarily have to be contained in one lifetime. He gave the example of someone agreeing as part of a life contract to become involved with drugs or alcohol in order to help someone else in the family group with his or her soul experience, because the addiction is linked with family genetics. Research by the National Institute on Drug Abuse[1] has shown that alcoholism runs in families, in support of John's statement.

Other spirits may have to "endure more than one lifetime to learn their lesson," which links them to the karma they have created by not facing their challenges. This is where the "tapestry of life" becomes very complex and not easily explained, even for those spirits who are observing and learning in the afterlife.

The idea of free will existing in association with destiny in these areas can be very confusing for some people. John gave the example of a person whose life path was not intended to include drug taking, but somehow still ended up becoming an addict. The path ahead may include either dying from an overdose, which would have widespread effects on family and friends, or conversely getting off the drugs, rehabilitating themselves, and going on to help others. The question of which path is free will and which is destiny cannot be easily answered, because each case is unique. The implication here for us is that we are not qualified to judge people in such cases, as the tapestry of life is too complicated for easy answers.

Synchronicity or serendipity can also play a vital role in the entwining of the tapestry threads around us. Sometimes key events in life are created by free will, other times through synchronicity, and in many cases the circumstances surrounding these events are created for us by the spirits who watch over us in the afterlife. There are teams of spirits constantly working to create situations on our behalf, such as chance meetings, or incredible opportunities that may well have been created just for us as part of our life contract, agreed to before we are born. A significant memory or an inspired thought may come out of the blue. Sometimes, somehow, we just *know* something and feel the need to follow a hunch or gut reaction.

Synchronicity is an ever-present reality for those who have eyes to see.

—CARL JUNG, 1875–1961

I've personally experienced destiny at work. Many years ago I went to Egypt to find Carol, a feisty English blonde whom I had met the week before in Greece. She did not know of my sudden decision, made on the spur of the moment on a cold, wet day in London. I knew the hotel at which she was supposedly holidaying in Cairo and, after being delayed at the airport in London for a couple of days, I finally arrived at first light on a hot Egyptian morning, with fingers crossed that Carol was still there.

My heart sank when the desk clerk said there was nobody with her name at the hotel. It began to look as if I had made the trip in vain. However, something made me glance down at the reception desk, where a pile of passports was waiting to be inspected by the police. Egypt was at war with Israel at the time, and all tourists had to surrender their passports for police examination. Much to my surprise, there, sitting on top of the pile, was Carol's passport, with her name prominently displayed. Serendipity at its best! When I excitedly pointed this out to the clerk, he became embarrassed as he was pronouncing the *w* in her surname as a *v*.

So with my heart pounding and a great sense of relief I prepared to surprise Carol. She answered the phone in a dazed voice and asked where I was calling from, then nearly dropped the receiver when I told her I was downstairs in reception. Needless to say, it was a very emotional reunion, albeit at six a.m.

Having connected again, we went on an amazing journey through an Egypt devoid of tourists because of the war with Israel. It was a once-in-a-lifetime opportunity to visit sites such as the Great Pyramid in Giza and the tombs of the pharaohs in the Valley of the Kings, which were almost deserted at the time. In the Cairo Museum, the mummies of several pharaohs were still on display just prior to being locked away from the public. As a lover of Egyptian history, I am very fortunate that my steps of destiny in reconnecting with Carol resulted in such wonderful experiences. However, it was not all sightseeing, and our romance blossomed as we adventured around this fascinating country. So much so that at the end of our time in Egypt, Carol agreed to come to Australia to live with me, and four years later we got married.

To this day I believe that unseen powers were pulling the strings that day, as our destiny was to reunite and work through karma from past lives. The other interesting part of that story was that while I was making inquiries about visiting Greece before leaving Australia, the general manager of the tour company involved recognized me from TV and immediately offered me a free seven-day holiday in Greece with no strings attached. The offer came out of nowhere, as all I was doing was inquiring about a tour brochure of classical Greece, which my mother, knowing my interest in history, had given to me.

On the other side of the world, Carol, who was a tour manager for the same travel company, had finished her contract for the year, but was persuaded to come back and conduct one more tour on classical Greece. Our team in spirit was very active in making sure we connected. In retrospect, there were so many pieces of the puzzle that had to come together that it was definitely a vital destiny point specifically created for both of us.

People in the spirit world observe, interact, and analyze life stories like this as part of their own ongoing soul growth, so this tapestry thread extends beyond the earth plane. An important part of their soul group work allows people to go back over their last life to examine in detail the whys and the hows, once again bringing the tapestry links into focus. John spoke about the regrets he had when he saw in his life review how his last lifetime was meant to play out, but was diverted by the choices he made: "I was put on earth in a position of power, but I became self-absorbed. I didn't use that position where I could have influenced a lot of people." He explained that he was given his abilities as a writer and journalist to teach and to help, but ego got in the way, and that was his downfall.

John is able to look back now and see how this affected his family relationships, how not having the courage to face his fears influenced his whole life. He now realizes that everything placed in his path was a part of his life contract that he was "supposed to deal with and overcome." John describes his early passing as the opportunity to still continue his unfulfilled life's work in spirit by working with me. Another thread in the tapestry.

The problems and situations we face in our lifetime do not simply disappear if we are unable to resolve them, so John knows that he is fortunate to be given another opportunity to complete his destiny. It is not like leaving work at the end of the day, realizing you have made a mistake. You know it is too late to do anything now, so you'll sort it out tomorrow. Major unresolved situations are often carried over into the next life, after we have carefully analyzed them in our between-life group sessions. We may have to learn how to handle them in a different way, but deal with them we must.

My romantic sojourn in Egypt turned out to be part of an ongoing saga from the dim, dark past. Once Carol and I had worked through our karma, the relationship began to sour and fade, and we eventually went our own ways. Five years later I consulted a visiting Indian mystic, who was adept at accessing the Akashic Records in the afterlife. These records hold all the details of every life we have ever lived and are stored in the Hall of Records in the afterlife. (See *Afterlife*, chapter 23, and chapter 38 of this book.) Although the mystic had never met either of us, he described Carol perfectly and told me that I had been instrumental in her accidental death in a previous life in Egypt, but the karma was now balanced. The meeting shed some light on the agonizing repercussions of what had become a toxic relationship, and I believe the mystic appeared in my life to explain why Carol and I had to connect again in this lifetime.

By this time I was with Judy, and the mystic told us both that we were part of the same soul family and it was our destiny to meet again at that stage of our lives. Our previous times together had mostly been fairly short, but were always intense and meaningful. We did not have any outstanding karmic issues to resolve, but had simply chosen to savor more time together again after sharing many past lives.

Complex situations may be thrown at us that were not part of our life plan, because not every single event that crops up in our life can be scheduled in spirit. These unexpected events are part of the tapestry of life and we often refer to them as "the six degrees of separation," meaning that everybody on earth can be connected through six introductions. Lately, though, I am finding many of my contacts closer to two degrees of separation!

Studies in areas such as astrology and numerology tell us that certain personal characteristics and major challenges may be part of the blueprint of life. I believe that these built-in abilities and challenges are part of the karmic contract that we agree to in spirit before entering each new body. A birth chart outlines the strengths and challenges each person has agreed to work with in that life, so there is a set of guidelines available to us here on earth if we choose to access them.

7

The Dangers of Negativity

We know all too well the effects negativity can have in every aspect of our lives. People who are always negative can be very hard to live with, and recent statistics showing the growth rate of depression in our society are very disturbing. It seems that all too often it is far easier to plunge into negative thinking and fear than to look for the silver lining in the dark clouds. This tendency to indulge in negativity is unfortunately compounded by certain elements of the media seemingly determined to fill news bulletins and current affairs programs with stories of violence, misfortune, and disasters. Good news stories are more often confined to the fluffy animal story at the end of the TV broadcast. A cynical observer may well think this is the spoonful of sugar needed to make the previous dose of medicine palatable.

I had thought that negativity would have been eliminated as part of life in the spirit world, but John soon dispelled that impression. Even in the afterlife, the power of negativity is recognized as a force to be dealt with. The potency of group energy there is used to help bring about change and send positive messages to those on earth. However, the power of destructive groups in spirit is acknowledged to have an even greater impact at times, because negativity is actually a stronger force. Even small groups projecting damaging energy can be more powerful than their larger, positive counterparts. This is because it is much easier to be negative, whereas it takes a lot more energy to be positive, strong, and loving. This once again reflects the continuing theme of "As above, so below."

Hatred and anger are such strong emotions that they can stay with people long after they cross over, and require an effort of will to release them. There are many levels or planes of existence in the world of spirit. Although all reports from the afterlife deny the existence of hell, spirits will cross over to their appropriate soul level. More on this in the next chapter. These spirits bring their unresolved negative emotions into the lower astral planes of the afterlife, where they must learn to recognize and shed them before being able to move to higher levels. To progress in the afterlife, we need to embrace love and positivity. If we find anger, hatred, jealousy, and similar feelings too difficult to release, then they are incorporated into the karma of our next incarnation. This explains why some people seem to be born with dark energy around them. They may also attract these negative emotions in the next life in order to learn firsthand the lessons associated with them.

John's group confirmed that there are indeed many beings from other worlds and other dimensions living among us on earth, some of whom are far more negative than we are. They spread their darkness as they mingle with us, often unintentionally, not necessarily trying to disrupt our lives, as their DNA is basically incompatible with ours.

Some of these beings "from other solar systems" go to the same world of spirit as us when they die, but John says there are none residing in his particular area. His knowledge of them is scant, as he does not have contact with them at this stage.

At this point John casually threw in an interesting tidbit of associated information about the way we reincarnate. Once we reach a certain level in the afterlife, we may be offered the opportunity to reincarnate on other worlds instead of returning to earth. However, John has been told that his future lies in earthly lives, at least for the time being.

> *Negativity is an addiction to the bleak shadow that lingers*
> *around every human form . . . you can transfigure*
> *negativity by turning it toward the light of your soul.*

> —JOHN O'DONOHUE
> *Anam Cara: A Book of Celtic Wisdom*[1]

8

At Home in the Afterlife

As I drove up the steep road to Kelly and Kristin's hilltop property for another trance session with John's group, I stopped and looked out over the rolling green countryside to the distant ocean, lost in appreciation of what the locals call "God's country." I wondered if even the beauty of the spirit world could surpass this magnificent landscape. Then I started to think about the location of the afterlife; we had established earlier that it is all around us, but I was determined to ask John for more information.

Describing the location of the afterlife is not easy, even for those residing there. Essentially, John said, it is on another plane of existence, and because contact with those on earth is difficult, this makes it feel distant to him. This difficulty is apparently going to eventually

change and become easier as the vibration level of human consciousness rises and the two dimensions move closer together. The world of
spirit vibrates at a much higher rate than does the earth plane, even
though both fundamentally occupy the same space, which explains
our difficulty in seeing the spirit world.

There are many levels or planes in the vast world of spirit. John
explained his current level cannot be defined by a number, but for
him it is rather more of a "knowing" where he is. He understands that
he could even progress to another stage without realizing it consciously. This means that even though we are directly connecting
with our soul family when we return to the afterlife, each spirit could
be at various stages of soul evolution and inhabiting different planes.
Perhaps it is similar to family and friends living in different suburbs
and socioeconomic situations in a big city, or even in other parts of the
country; their lifestyles would reflect their experience and status in
society. John believes the reason that there are no numbers delineat-
ing each level is because they would only create competition, which
goes against the concept of life in the spirit world.

However, John was a little vague when it came time to discuss the
location of the advanced beings who are his teachers. My impression
was that he simply realized and accepted that they were many levels
above him, without knowing where and even how they actually lived,
as this was not relevant to their great wisdom. Similarly, it is irrelevant to our relationship with, and none of our concern, to know where
our university lecturer or boss lives.

Professor Frederic Myers, who founded the first Society for

Psychical Research in England in 1882, sent back concise information about the afterlife after he crossed over in 1901. Myers described the various planes in detail, which I have described in *Afterlife*. It would seem to me that John initially went to what Myers labeled "the Plane of Illusion," to which the vast majority of us return in between lives. There are many sublevels within this plane, so it makes sense that we can raise ourselves to higher levels as our soul develops, without necessarily being ushered through a gateway or given some graduation certificate with a golden key attached. My guide M informed me that our guides in the afterlife will quietly let us know when we advance ourselves, something we keep private. Boasting of our achievements is frowned upon, as the competitive streak that is so much a part of life on earth is unnecessary in the afterlife.

Advanced beings could come from the highest levels of "the Plane of Illusion" as well as from the other planes described by Myers, the next one being "the World of Idealized Form." This is where the soul, no longer needing to reincarnate, explores avenues beyond the confines and illusions of the earth plane.

John described these advanced beings as often appearing in human form when they visit the lower planes, usually projecting a male energy as far as he is able to gauge. However, this is a matter of personal recognition and depends on what kind of individual perception is required at that time. When he first returned to the afterlife, John needed to see spirits projecting an earthly appearance to support his own belief system. He wanted to see their lips moving and hear words coming from their mouths. This requirement soon diminished and he became content to just be in their presence. After a while he was able to understand their thoughts without seeing their lips moving or hearing their words. The next stage was to release the need for appearances and to simply "be in energy with them."

He revealed, though, that the deep need to see someone in human form has not entirely left him. When he first meets a new spirit he is curious to see what he looks like in physical form, to put a face to the voice. John said this is completely unnecessary, but it is still a foible he has yet to release.

Normally spirits appear to one another as "a ball of light, or pure energy." John described the feeling of being surrounded by energy, and explained that all communication at this stage is done by thought. This also can be achieved from a distance, as spirits do not have to be in the same place together to have a conversation. The quality of this depends on many things, such as the individual level of advancement, how much you want to hang on to the image of the human body, and how long you have been back in the afterlife. This also helps to explain how people in the afterlife are able to communicate with those on earth, mostly via mediums, although spirits can learn to lower their vibrations so that they can be seen.

John said people cannot return to the afterlife and expect to have great conversations with other spirits from the moment they arrive. We start off simply, with basic communication skills, and then it takes patience and practice. It is much like learning another language, according to my guide M. This also can depend on how spiritually advanced we are on arrival and how many lifetimes we have had.

At this point John reiterated that one of the hardest habits to drop when we return to the world of spirit is that of referring and relating to time. In our sessions he made frequent references to time, which he said were necessary for us to relate to his descriptions of events and situations in the afterlife. It can make communicating with us difficult when it comes to making plans, as spirits have to consciously put themselves back into earthly habits. It also explains why we are not always able to connect with those in the afterlife when it suits us, even though we may have set up a meeting with a medium beforehand. However, more often than not, people in the afterlife are only too pleased to take any opportunity to communicate with loved ones back on earth.

So when you next get guidance from someone in spirit, it is best not to ask too many questions about the timing surrounding the advice. M informs me that this particularly applies when we are asking for help from our guides. The timing of our actions is an earthly event, and is up to us to work out for ourselves.

Apart from his own work and activities in the afterlife, one of John's favorite pastimes is looking over the welfare of family and loved ones on earth, sending them guidance whenever possible. He sees them often struggling with everyday life and its stressful situations, realizing from his perspective that they are putting themselves through unnecessary worries and stress. Everything really does get resolved in the end and worry does not help the process, but in fact hinders it. Fear often forces people to make wrong decisions, and those in spirit encourage us to concentrate on love instead so that we can surmount these fears.

9

Sport and the Afterlife

Rugby—the game they play in heaven.

—POPULAR SAYING DATING BACK TO THE 1980S

One of my favorite memories from my career as a radio and TV presenter is cohosting a sports program on TV for several years. I have always been a great sports lover, though my talents on the sporting field leave a lot to be desired. This interest gave me several years anchoring a weekly telecast that covered just about every sport in the book. I also got to host a Commonwealth Games TV coverage in New Zealand and was the studio anchor for an Olympic Games broadcast. Nowadays I am happy to follow sports such as cricket and all football codes as a spectator while each week waving a tennis racquet around, pretending I'm playing tennis.

Spirits in the afterlife are able to pursue any number of relaxation activities, from cultural to sporting. As everything in the world of spirit is created with the power of thought, it is very easy to go swimming, climb mountains, play tennis, go horseback riding, or create a round of golf on a stunning golf course that is literally out of this world. It is also possible, through thought and memory, to enjoy the experience of an actual event of the past, such as your favorite football final or even one of the great Olympic Games.

But what about those people who were avid supporters of a sporting team while they were living their last life? We all know about the fans that week after week travel around, following their football, cricket, basketball, or baseball team. Some groups even take time off work to follow their national team when it tours to other countries. The legendary "Barmy Army," which vociferously follows the English cricket team around the world, is made up of fans from various social and professional backgrounds. What happens to these often manic supporters when they return to the afterlife? Do they have to wistfully leave it all behind as a distant memory?

Definitely not, according to John Dingwall: Spirits are keen to follow their teams from the afterlife just as they did on earth.

Whatever sport you loved during your life on earth remains with you in the afterlife for as long as you wish. Over the course of time this interest may fade, but it is obviously not considered a problem by the powers that be in spirit.

John said he still has a yearning for the sport of rugby, which he enjoyed in his last life, and admitted he often popped back to earth to watch a game. Sporting venues, it would appear, may have much bigger crowds than show up on official figures. "The higher profile the sporting event, the more spirits are in attendance," John said. And they get in free!

He went on to make a very interesting observation about the high level of excitement frequently achieved on earth during great sporting events such as the Olympic Games or the FIFA World Cup. For many people, everything else in their life disappears as they completely focus on the action of the event, and he described it as almost like connecting with spirit. He also added that it can be something like rebirthing.

So I'm looking forward to creating a sub-par round on a magnificent celestial golf course when I return and will also, at last, have the perfect backhand in tennis. Such blissful afterlife dreams are made of this!

10

Judy's Surprise

The sudden passing of my partner Judy in 1997 had an incredible effect on my life, at first devastating and then enlightening. Judy and I realized shortly after we met that we had a very deep soul contact, but after only four short years together she disappeared from my life. Or so I thought.

With the help of medium Ruth Phillips (née Wilson), I was able to establish contact with Judy in the afterlife a few months after she passed, an event that not only opened up my medium abilities, but ultimately provided the inspiration for me to write my first book. In the years following her death, Judy kept giving me spiritual jabs to get moving and write. These messages were passed on from different sources in various parts of the world, including one from Canadian medium Robert Murray after he had appeared on *Radio Out There*. This further proves the many ways our loved ones are able to communicate with us in spirit.

Ruth kindly agreed to also be part of this story, and her contact with Judy, detailed in chapter 55 of this book, has helped me complete a very important life transformation.

However, Judy had earlier decided that she wanted to have a more direct contribution to this book, and took the opportunity to come through to me at one of my talks. On this occasion I was scheduled to speak in the morning session, and after lunch the presenter was visiting UK medium Val Hood, who had appeared on my radio program earlier that year while on a visit to Australia. Val has a wonderful reputation in Great Britain, where she has appeared as a medium in gatherings ranging from spiritual churches to large theaters, winning over audiences wherever she goes. Val has now moved to Australia, having fallen in love with this country, and will be a great asset to the community.

Just prior to my talk I got a very clear message from Spirit that Judy would speak to me later that day through Val. This was very surprising, because it felt as if I had lost contact with Judy in recent months, and I'd wondered if she had moved on to higher things once my book was published.

My own talk went much like the many others I had given that year. Once I begin speaking about the afterlife, Spirit just takes over, my mind goes into overdrive, and the words pour out of my mouth, surprising even me at times. Sometimes it feels as if I am channeling the information. I keep remembering John Dingwall's words that the powers that be in the world of spirit are on a concerted drive to let as many people as possible know that there is no such thing as death. They are determined to remove as much fear as possible about our natural progression in life. Communicators all over the world are being inspired to spread the word, and I firmly believe Spirit takes every opportunity and method to help get its message across.

Val is a highly experienced conscious medium who goes far beyond simply giving "survival evidence." Many mediums can provide enough evidence to prove they are in contact with the spirit of the deceased, but are unable to receive further information. Val's bubbly personality breaks down any barriers that may exist with her audiences as she connects closely with the spirit energy that she brings through. The messages just flow through her mind, and she passes on the kind of specific information that people are often desperate to receive from loved ones in the spirit world.

That afternoon the room was packed, but you could have heard the proverbial pin drop as Val described the first spirit that was communicating with her. I knew immediately it was Judy, and my heart missed a couple of beats.

Val accurately described Judy's appearance and personality in her last life, despite having never met or even seen a picture of her. Nor had she read my book. Val went on to give me many different messages over the next fifteen minutes or so, much to my delight. Judy finished by saying it was about time I started my next book. Up to that point I had been doing a lot of communicating with John Dingwall and the team but had not so much as written a title page.

To cap off her very personal message, Judy told me word for word what John had said in a trance session a few months prior. My head began to spin; I could not believe what I was hearing. Val did not know anything about John and his team, let alone details of our contact sessions. This was the kind of synchronicity that proved to me beyond a doubt that it was indeed Judy speaking through Val. Not that I needed convincing, but I am human, and sometimes seeds of doubt can creep into my mind. The emotional impact of the contact with Judy really hit home, and afterward I had to leave the room to recover. Speaking with Val afterward, I discovered that she, too, was close to tears during Judy's very emotional contact.

That was it. I left that afternoon, determined to start writing the next book. A week later I began listening to several recordings of recent trance sessions with John Dingwall, and suddenly I was off and away with this book. The story started to flow a lot easier than I had imagined.

In going through the recordings again I found a reference that I had forgotten, in which John said he was in touch with Judy. She is part of the group supporting him as he channels, providing both energy and information as part of the collective. He also mentioned that when the time was right, Judy would come through personally.

I guess she figured a prod from Spirit was necessary to get me moving again.

Thanks, Jude, I obviously needed that.

Surprise is the greatest gift which life can grant us.

—BORIS PASTERNAK, 1890–1960,
winner of the Nobel Prize in Literature, 1958

11

Group Discussions in the Afterlife

As a child I used to imagine that people in heaven lazed around on clouds, strumming harps, surrounded by angels and cherubs fluttering by, and generally enjoying themselves with not a care in the world. I'm not sure whether that was the picture created in Sunday-school lessons, or just part of my generation's "Walt Disney" image of the celestial world. I don't wish to be iconoclastic, but at the risk of repeating myself, nothing could be further from the truth. The concept of being toasted in the fiery pits of hell is also a myth, thank heavens, along with some bearded guy in a red suit, sporting horns and a tail and wielding a ghastly pitchfork.

Once we have returned home to the world of spirit and our healing is completed, hopefully removing the imprint of our last life's mal-aises, we rejoin our soul groups and our spiritual development contin-ues. This is achieved in many cases through group learning sessions, often similar to our school or university days. Advanced beings or teachers are there to help each group, and a lot of discussion and anal-ysis take place, usually in informal situations.

Those in spirit can also maintain close links with activities on earth, on both a personal and community level. To emphasize a previ-ous point, spirits are not allowed to interfere in our lives, but once given permission by the guides, they can make subtle suggestions and influences, using the power of thought communication, dreams, signs, and many other means.

Not only is this contact on a personal level, but the influence from Spirit can have a larger impact on earthly life. John Dingwall spoke of the current concern in the spirit realms of the deteriorating relation-ship between the Eastern and Western nations. They have many dis-cussions in spirit about the number of potential conflicts, with many countries on the brink of war at any one time. Their big concern is that in a lot of these troubled areas, particularly in the Middle East, many people have "nothing to lose and everything to gain" in their battle against the West, which makes it so difficult for everyone involved. While adhering to their policy of non-interference, John said, there is "a huge push" by spirits working on influential leaders to offer guidance and help in areas of tolerance and understanding with other countries. He also acknowledged the influence of religions in this situation, saying that religious organizations on earth are far more powerful than many of us realize.

The question of potential intervention from the spirit world is also a hot topic in the afterlife. An important point raised in these discussions is that in most cases events must be allowed to run their course, "so that people can learn their lessons out of the hardship that comes from making their mistakes."

John gave the example of a sick child suffering and finally dying amid grief and anger, with people saying, "If there is a God, how could he let this happen?" Hard as it may be for the family concerned, the other side of the story is the good that may come from such a death. Lives can change as a result of the child's passing, with parents starting reform groups or medical science being triggered to find answers. These things happen for a reason. In the case of huge conflicts in the world, a positive result may occur when countries band together to make changes.

Another popular topic of discussion in the afterlife is the syndrome of instant gratification in today's world. People want a quick fix to their problems, which is why many of them rely so heavily on gurus, media experts, psychics, and other instantly available resources, instead of going within themselves for their answers. The concern is that too many people are losing their patience; if things are not done immediately, they want to know why. They are not looking for answers in their head or in their heart; it is much easier to find the solution on the Internet. This applies particularly to children and young people who are taking the easy way out, using technology instead of thinking about the whole question. This kind of escapism can be damaging in the long term.

Author Helen Brown defines this syndrome beautifully in her book *After Cleo Came Jonah*.[1] She describes meandering through "a sea of impassive faces . . . bent over little boxes, white wires dangling from their ears, attached to realities that didn't exist. Connected to the abstract but disconnected from their living."

The apprehension in the afterlife is that our complete reliance on technology is a potential problem and may be found to be disruptive to everyday life in a huge way in the not too distant future. If computers around the world suddenly crash, for whatever reason, our lives would be thrown into chaos. When I thought about how reliant we have become on computers, the impact made my head spin. Everything from basic everyday needs, such as food and fuel distribution, water and communications to banking, commerce, air travel, and utility organizations are highly dependent on computer technology. The list goes on and on—no wonder they are concerned for us in the afterlife.

The Elders in the world of spirit sent a special message via John's team that they are troubled about the way we are generally handling world affairs and the environment. They said we are living in a "strange time" in which we are on the cusp of some wonderful spiritual advances but are being adversely affected by greed, materialism, and lack of concern for others. Our young people are not building a solid base to sustain themselves, with their constant need for instant gratification through material possessions, self-image, and technology.

The problem is, instant gratification takes too long. . . .

—MERYL STREEP AS SUZANNE IN
Postcards from the Edge

12

The Body Beautiful

After I took a two-month break from writing over the festive season it was difficult to get out of holiday mode and get started again, despite Judy's words of encouragement. I live in a tropical coastal area, and the summer weather is more conducive to being laid-back than industrious. Feeling blocked, I put out a request to my guide M for inspiration and motivation, and received a very clear dream message to meditate with the two large crystals I had obtained while at John of God's healing center in Brazil. These crystals, which I wrote about in *Afterlife*, were a special gift from John of God himself, and helped me raise my vibrations and connect with higher realms, and this was an obvious solution to my new year's lethargy. All I needed was a spiritual boot in the backside!

M was waiting for me once I went deep into meditation using the crystals, and our communication resumed.

While we have free will to conduct our lives as we choose, those in spirit are always sending us messages to guide us whenever we need it, but it also helps to ask for guidance when we are in a quandary. Most of the time we are too busy with our daily lives to listen to our spirit helpers, but they never seem to become impatient with us. Their guidance can take many subtle forms—dreams, signs that have a personal meaning, a flash of inspiration, or even a song on the radio. In the months after Judy passed over, I would sometimes pause and wonder where she was at that moment. On a couple of occasions her favorite song, "I Will Survive," suddenly came on the car radio; once I was so overwhelmed, I was forced to pull over to a side street, tears pouring down my face. It was the perfect survival evidence I needed. On other occasions Joe Cocker's song "You Are So Beautiful" would be played at a very appropriate moment. I knew Judy was there with me, as this was the song I played for her at her funeral.

Sometimes Spirit needs to get through to us in a more dramatic fashion when it is obvious that we are not taking heed, such as when we lose a job, or have a relationship break up. Our guides and spirit helpers know that we will be forced to be introspective at these transformational times in our life, and they have a better chance of getting through to us. A friend of mine who practices numerology receives messages from license plates of nearby cars when she is looking for guidance, which has proved very reliable over the years.

Our guides can only offer advice; they cannot do it for us, as that would defeat the purpose of our life. However, they usually gently steer us along certain paths so that we can link with our destiny points in each lifetime. This can result in what we often regard as chance meetings, coincidences, being in the right place at the right time, and, of course, encountering people and events that change our lives. M had already confirmed that while we have free will, there are certain destiny points that we have agreed to in spirit as we prepare for each incarnation.

Another growing concern the Elders in the afterlife have for us is our infatuation with our physical image to the detriment of our spiritual growth. While those who could afford it have always been concerned with fashion and personal appearance through the ages, it is now getting out of proportion, particularly in Western societies. The "body beautiful" is for many people a lifelong obsession.

Everything has beauty, but not everyone sees it.

—CONFUCIUS, 550–479 BCE

To illustrate this point, M showed me a vision of a weekly newspaper I usually read that has a section called "Body and Soul." For a long time I used to play a game of "hunt for the soul stories," which are usually swamped by articles and advice about body image, diet tips, recipes, beauty products, weight-loss programs, and the like, with just a token soul-related article and the obligatory astrology column. After a while I gave it up as a fruitless exercise. Of course, commercial media content is all dependent on advertising, with stories about our physical image attracting the dollars, while sadly there are not many major advertisers queuing up to sponsor spiritual features. In fact, most mainstream media coverage seems to ignore or simply ridicule spiritual and metaphysical stories, which goes a long way toward explaining public apathy to these subjects.

An image of a motor vehicle flashed into my mind with the message that our love of cars reflects this situation. Many people are so obsessed with their cars, to the detriment of other aspects of their life, that they can lose perspective of their vehicle's basic purpose.

As M pointed out, a car is merely a vehicle for transportation, and needs the energy of our presence behind the wheel to put it into motion. He compared this to our physical bodies, which are merely vehicles for our spirit to experience each lifetime. The key point he made is that our spiritual energy is the main reason that the body was created in the first place. Sure, we need to keep our vehicle well maintained, but the spirit, which is eternal, will outlast the body that is allocated to us in each lifetime. Passing over is akin to trading in your old vehicle, which has outlived its purpose, and waiting for the appropriate replacement.

Understanding and developing the power that lies at our very heart is vital over the longer term of our life. To do this we need to go inside our "vehicle" far more than we do, and not just concern ourselves primarily with polishing the outer casing. Exploring our spiritual depths takes a conscious effort, and it is far easier to look in the mirror to make ourselves feel good and be presentable to the world at large. What we do not always take into account is that, apart from a few close friends and family, the vast majority of people we see every day are not really concerned with what we are wearing or how we look, unless we draw attention to ourselves through such things as unseemly behavior, body piercing, or ugly tattoos. They are mostly too busy thinking about their own image and worrying about what we think about *them* to pay much notice to our appearance.

Our outer body will age with the years, but the inner riches we all possess will always stay fresh and new, constantly updating and improving with age and experience. Our soul has every answer that we ever need safely locked inside. When we open our heart and connect with our soul through meditation, the power of the spirit world is available to us. We all possess intuition; we just need to learn to access and trust it. After all, intuition basically means learning from within.

Using your intuition can help you every day in many basic ways, but does not mean you have to become a psychic to be able to use it. As I was leaving to go to the bank today I heard that the town was very crowded, traffic was really hectic, and it would be very difficult to park. I tuned in to my inner knowing and asked for assistance and visualized a parking spot in a particular street just around the corner from the bank. Trusting my inner knowing, I drove straight there, and, lo and behold, that exact empty spot was waiting for me.

By accessing and trusting our inner knowing, we can all find anything from a simple parking spot to our purpose in life, and indeed much more.

Part Two

The Mists of Time

13

M Speaks Up

If you want to know your past life, look into your present condition; if you want to know your future life, look at your present actions.

—PADMASAMBHAVA,
eighth-century Tibetan sage

The wonderful thing about my guide M is that he is always there for me when I need his sage advice. I doubt that I could have written my first book without his guidance. One night before going to sleep I put a question to him about what was important to include in this book. I awoke the next morning with his answer ringing in my mind. "Investigate another of your past lives and between-life experiences."

M had already guided me through my most recent past life as Brian, something I wrote about in *Afterlife*. So many people who read the book have identified with Brian's between-life soul journey, so M's suggestion hardly came as a surprise. He was probably shaking his head, metaphorically speaking, wondering why I hadn't thought of it myself.

There is a popular saying that you need to make the most of this life, as "you only live once." However, when we start to research the fascinating subject of reincarnation, the facts are hard to dispute. A multitude of evidence has proved to me that reincarnation is a natural part of the life cycle of human beings. Once we accept that we are a spiritual energy powering a human body, it is easy to understand that our physical form is our vehicle for an earthly experience. When the body perishes, the spirit returns to the world of spirit, where it originally came from, and here it goes through a rest and reevaluation period before embarking on another adventure.

During this intervening period, many spirits in the afterlife can access other lives they have led, as part of their ongoing education program. When given permission by their guides, they are able to view the Akashic Records, which are stored in the Hall of Records. Far from being a kind of TV show, they are interactive, as people experience for themselves the effects their activities and behavior in past lives have had on others they have encountered. It is a very important part of our soul development in the afterlife. We are obliged to "feel" the emotional pain that we have caused others so that we can take full responsibility for our actions. Especially if we managed to avoid these responsibilities in our last earth life.

When the timing is right, it is always delightful to see things fall into place smoothly. I believe in synchronicity, as opposed to coincidence, and it was working well for me in this instance. I was telling Belinda Grace, a clairvoyant and author who has appeared on my radio program *Radio Out There*, about my regression plans, saying that I was looking for a good past-life therapist. Belinda immediately recommended that I ring Colleen, a past-life and between-life regression therapist, with whom she had reconnected only the day before. Surprise, surprise!

When I contacted Colleen, she told me that she had been trained in the Michael Newton method as well as being a qualified hypnotherapist. Michael Newton, the author of books such as *Journey of Souls*, has developed an international training program for "life between lives" therapy.

We agreed that it would be best if Colleen did not read *Afterlife*, as it could influence the way she conducted my regression. The only details I gave her were that I wanted to visit a past life or lives, relevant to my research and current life, and then follow my spirit through on each occasion as it returned into the afterlife.

Colleen told me it would probably be about a four-hour session, starting midmorning, and to eat a good breakfast that day to sustain me. I wasn't sure at the time whether she thought we might go back to a turbulent time when I would need all the strength I could muster.

Maybe even visit a life where I died of starvation. Anyway, I ate a hearty breakfast before heading off for my regression. I'm glad I took her advice, as it turned out to be quite an exhausting session.

Many people think having a past-life regression would be a fun thing to do, a kind of Hollywood time-tunnel experience. However, a trained therapist will usually perform a regression only to provide answers to questions and situations that may be causing blockages or major concerns in their current life, or, as was my case, to answer relevant questions about their life path.

Some of the experts in the field of past-life research originally stumbled upon this form of therapy accidentally, while trying to find answers to emotional and physical problems in their patients' lives. One of Australia's pioneers in this field, Peter Ramster, a clinical psychologist, asked his patient under hypnosis to go back to a time in life when the problem first began. Peter was perplexed when his patient went back several hundred years, to a previous life. His initial skepticism melted away when the patient not only identified the cause of her problem, but subsequently started healing. Realizing he was onto something that could benefit many others, Peter encouraged other clients to use hypnotherapy to discover the source of their problems. A man of many talents, he was so delighted with the results of this therapy that he went on to produce two television specials, called *The Reincarnation Experiments*, which have been screened worldwide. Peter also wrote a book, *The Search for Lives Past*, and is now regarded as a leader in this field.

I was tempted to ask Peter to perform a regression for my research, but as he is a good friend and was working with Judy before she passed, I felt it best to work with a therapist with whom I have no personal connection. It would ensure that any information I was able to access was 100 percent genuine and could not be influenced in any subconscious way by the practitioner. Little did I realize the surprises that were in store for me as we swept aside the mists of time.

14

Down the Time Tunnel

To be able to enjoy one's past life is to live twice.

—MARCUS AURELIUS, ROMAN EMPEROR, 161–180 CE

As I drove to Colleen's rooms I was feeling a little apprehensive about the session. Four hours is a long time to be sitting in a chair in a state of hypnosis, and none of my previous sessions had been nearly as long.

The big question playing in my mind was where would I go in the regression? I had already asked M to ensure that I did not revisit my time as Brian, as that would have been a waste of energy. Knowing that I have had many lives as a warrior, I wondered if I would once again end up with a sword or a spear in my hands in some bloody battle.

A typical past-life regression starts with being taken back gradually in a very relaxed state similar to meditation, beginning with memories from early times in this life to get the subconscious mind moving in the right direction. Once we are in deep trance, our higher self, the part of the soul that is not attached to the physical body, is able to communicate directly with the therapist.

Initially I went back to early childhood and enjoyed some memories from those innocent days. I was raised in a loving family situation, typical of postwar times. My father had been away combating the Japanese invaders, and I did not meet him until I was three years of age. He was a very quiet, conservative man who was always there to support his family, although sadly he and I never really became as close as I would have liked, perhaps because of the early separation. Not surprisingly, my mother and I were much closer. I had a very innocent childhood and, apart from some bullying incidents when I first went to school, it was a happy time that I looked back on.

Once in a blissful state of mind and body, I was taken back to my time in the womb. Initially I felt very cramped, but was relieved that I didn't have to stay there as the fetus grew; my spirit could come and go quite happily. When asked where I went, I replied, "Back home." I also explained that, at first, I came into my new body when I needed to get to know my mother, which felt like about six months into the pregnancy.

The return "home" was mainly to communicate with my guide to do last-minute preparation for the life ahead. I also was able to spend some time with my soul family and say my farewells to them before joining the new body full-time. Other research that I have done into the time we have in the womb shows that most souls come and go during the pregnancy, with some only finally committing to joining the body fully just before birth. As with all afterlife experiences, each person's story is unique. Some souls like to be with their new mother for long periods in a kind of bonding time. M tells me that other souls choose to enjoy a rest period in the womb before birth, often because they are about to have a very hectic life ahead.

Meanwhile back with "little Barry" in the womb, I described the feeling as "not a new experience, but a little strange after the freedom of the spirit world to be contained in a tiny, tiny body."

I was asked to connect with my soul energy, sometimes referred to as the "oversoul" but mainly known as the higher self. The aim was to identify what I had been told in spirit, as it would be important in the new life about to unfold. My soul energy replied, "To learn and grow." Other themes then emerged: the word *communicate* was important, as was the idea of having fun this time around. There would also be many lessons to learn around relationships.

I was able to recall some of my "soul briefing," during which my guide had told me that it was important for me to be born at that time, in the middle of World War II, as I had a lot of past history around war and fighting. This lifetime had a feeling of being connected to a war but at the same time I did not have to be part of it, beyond the early environment.

My previous between-life experience as Brian, described in *After-life*, revealed that I had completed my experiences as a warrior and had finally accepted the huge waste that war created. An important part of this next life was to help people understand the futility of war, as well as to gain further understanding for myself of the waste and human degradation it created.

The information from my higher self during this womb time kept on coming. The reason I had experienced so many past lives as a warrior was "a deep-seated anger that needed to be released." Indeed, there were still some karmic aspects around anger that would need to be worked through in this life, but this would play out around relationships instead of war. I also chose this body, even though it had eye problems, because of the experiences that were in store for me in this life. I had to discover and *see* things for myself. This lifetime would also be much longer than several of my previous ones, which were cut short for various reasons.

The date and time of my birth were chosen for me and have "a deep significance" and will help my soul in this life.

The question of lives in other worlds arose in my soul briefing, but so far I have chosen to learn my lessons on earth; maybe I will graduate to other worlds for future lives. My soul energy acknowledged an intention to experience another world, and when further questioned replied that I would like to experience a world of peace, a life where there would be a more loving environment. There are apparently many such worlds in the universe.

My soul energy sent a message to Barry in the present time saying, "Get it all done." Achievements and experiences are all important in this lifetime, but above all make sure of completions.

With that helpful message about my life as Barry, I was then immersed into a deeper part of my soul memory to continue the exploration into other incarnations.

Listening back a couple of months later to the recording of this very long regression, I was constantly amazed by the detailed information that emerged from my subconscious soul memory. Many of the events and conclusions were completely different from what I had anticipated beforehand, and the details about my past lives were intense.

Before my regression I was fully expecting that I would be going back to a time in ancient Egypt or Rome, which are two of my favorite periods of history, but it was not to be. I certainly did not anticipate a life in the wilds of a jungle.

15

Meeting Kalingah

I slipped easily into a past lifetime, and when prompted heard my name being called. It sounded like "Kalingah." I *looked down* in my mind's eye and saw I had the slender brown legs of a woman, wearing sandals on my feet and a kind of dress that ended below my knees. I was not asked to describe her facial or body features, but I had the feeling that she was small of stature and slight in build. At the time I connected with Kalingah she had been on earth for "twenty-two summers" and was preparing for some kind of ceremony. I strongly felt I was in a jungle area of South America and the year was 740. There was an active volcano near the village where she lived.

Kalingah had long, dark hair and was wearing a simple type of indigenous jewelry around her neck and wrists for the purpose of the ritual. It was described as "a kind of marriage ceremony, not to another person, but to a deity."

The name of the god to whom Kalingah was being bound sounded to me like "Baal," and she had been chosen for the honor as a child by the high priest in agreement with her father, who was the tribal chief. For many years prior to the ceremony, Kalingah had been learning and preparing for this day. She had to learn the beliefs of her religion as well as all the invocations, and pray to the gods every day.

It had been decided that Kalingah would also be a healer, so she was taught the healing arts by a very old "wise woman." This included mixing the potions made from herbs and many other ingredients found in the jungle. At times healers also used small amounts of animal blood as part of the mix. Each potion had to "look and smell right" and had to be accompanied by the appropriate prayers for it to be successful. So Kalingah had to learn the exact words to use in healing to bring in the power of the gods, which she was adamant were a very important part of the process. She also learned how to communicate with the ancestors in the spirit world as part of her training. There was also an ethical side to these teachings that needed to be embraced if they were to be successful. Healing needed to be for the highest good of all concerned.

Kalingah emphasized that she was not special, and that there were others who were also trained by the wise woman in the art of healing. After the ceremony Kalingah was formally recognized as a healer and was then able to work independently, visiting other areas nearby to help the sick. However, she never lost contact with the wise woman who remained her mentor.

When asked how she felt about being a healer, Kalingah replied simply, "It is my destiny, it is what I must do." Kalingah enjoyed helping people, especially children, and this made her life much more enjoyable. Kalingah said that because she had committed to a life of service, she could never have a marriage partner or bear children.

Part of her duties as a healer also involved working with people when they died, preparing the body and then helping conduct the ceremony—a life celebration that included much dancing—after which the bodies were burned. Kalingah had to make a mask for the dead person to wear in the death ceremony to help them "say goodbye and go from this life to the next." The mask also helped the families in their grief, as it was an important part of the ceremony conducted by the priest.

Each mask was unique to the person who had just died and was burned with the body. Kalingah described the creative process for each mask as being intuitive. She would close her eyes, and an image of the appropriate mask would be given to her by the gods and the spirits of the ancestors of the deceased. This visualization was also part of the training that Kalingah underwent before her graduation ceremony.

Kalingah always knew she was destined to be a healer. When she was very young her grandmother died, and she was fascinated by the death ceremony, especially her mask, and Kalingah wanted to know more. In many ways she felt that was the start of her apprenticeship and that this childhood interest could have been part of the reason that she was chosen by the priest.

Life in the village was simple, even for the family of the chieftain. Her mother's days were spent cooking and looking after the children. Kalingah did not see her mother very often while she was training, as she lived away from her family in a special area with the other tribal members being trained. This was the priest's domain and was sacrosanct. Following the ceremony, Kalingah said, she would be given her own place to live, where she would also conduct her healings. Finally being recognized as a healer made Kalingah feel very proud, although she still believed she had much to learn. This would come from experience and also with the ongoing help from the wise woman. "I will take the knowledge that I get from healing one [person] to help another."

When I later connected with my guide M, he told me that Kalingah was in fact living in Central America and not South America, as I had first thought. With my interest whetted, I decided to do some research on volcanic activity in this region and discovered that there had been an explosive eruption in the volcano bordering the lake in Arenal in Central America around the time of 750 CE.

My research also verified the use of ceremonial masks by jungle tribes, such as Kalingah described, particularly in special rituals such as funerals.

While I was not completely sure that the name of the deity I was given in the regression was in fact Baal, could it be possible that he was worshiped in some form by one or more of the tribes in Central America? The question intrigued me, and once again I decided to do a little more research.

Baal was the ancient god of rain, thunder, and lightning, whose worship went back as far as 1450 BCE. The observance of Baal extended from the Canaanites to the Phoenicians in the ancient world. Recent studies into the amazing seafaring expeditions of the Phoenicians indicate they could well have visited the Americas as part of their trading voyages. A review of a new book in *Nexus* magazine by Ruth Parnell six months after my regression caught my attention. *The Lost Worlds of Ancient America*, edited by Frank Joseph,[1] presents "overwhelming evidence that the Americas were visited by seafaring cultures going back at least four thousand years and continuing till not long before Columbus's voyage to the New World." The book goes on to mention that the depiction of corn in some Egyptian artworks suggests a little-known New World link.

Baal was also deified in ancient Egypt, where his name was translated as "lord or owner," and was also a famous deity in Memphis. Traces of cocoa and nicotine have also been found in some Egyptian mummies, leading to further speculation that there was contact between Egypt and the Americas. Cocoa and nicotine were indigenous to the Americas, and, according to the history books, not introduced to Africa until post-Columbian times.

Another possibility also considered by many researchers is that

Polynesian seafarers visited the Americas in ancient times. They, too, could have brought the worship of foreign gods to those shores from their earlier contacts.

However strange it seems on the surface, it remains well within the realms of possibility that the worship of Baal made it to the Americas from another ancient civilization. Perhaps Baal's association with thunder and lightning would have appealed to certain superstitious tribes living in the shadow of active volcanoes.

After this research, I realized that my soul's memories of Kalingah's village felt a lot more familiar and comfortable. I was ready to explore the next part of Kalingah's life.

16

────────── ⌒⌒ ──────────

Kalingah's Life Unfolds

I was guided forward in my regression and next connected with Kalingah after she had lived for "over thirty summers" and was engaged in preparing the mask for her father's funeral ceremony. Kalingah had confused feelings at his passing, sadness mixed with the happy knowledge that he was now joining his ancestors. She described her father as a good man who had helped many people, but his time had come, as it does for us all. When asked whether he was familiar to anyone in my life today, Kalingah identified him as the spirit of my close friend Roger, who is also part of my soul family.

Kalingah's younger brother Lim, as the eldest son in the family, took over the role of chief of the village with the blessing of the people, and she was pleased for him. At this stage of Kalingah's life she was working in association with mainly the priest and had little to do with her brother in his new role. Kalingah identified Lim as being my son Matthew in this lifetime.

Since she started working as a healer, Kalingah said, she had learned much and helped many people. While she had not been able to heal everyone, she had the confidence of the people and maintained, "It is important they believe."

The village where she lived was, for her times, of medium size, which she described as perhaps housing several hundred people. In the seven years since she had graduated, word of Kalingah's healing abilities had spread and she occasionally traveled away from her village for several days at a time, helping people in neighboring areas. While she was unable to marry and bear children because of the vows she had taken for her healing work, Kalingah assisted in the birthing of children, as well as their postnatal care. She was also now a teacher and trained several young girls who worked and traveled with her. She stressed the importance of teaching: "If something happens to me, there must be others to take my place." Her relationship with the priest had changed, as now she was essentially a healer and did not participate in religious ceremonies as she had during her training.

However, she retained her association with the funeral rites and found great satisfaction from painting the death masks. "Masks are a very important part of our life, not just for funerals," she said. "They help us honor the gods, but also importantly they enable us to say on our mask what is in our heart. The masks are only used in ceremony, telling others who we are and sometimes letting us know who we are ourselves as well."

What we have done for ourselves alone, dies with us;
what we have done for others and the world, remains
and is immortal.

—ALBERT PIKE, 1809–1891,
teacher and writer

Kalingah liked to carefully focus her energies, and spoke of completing her father's mask before returning to her healing work. She preferred to focus on one thing at a time so that she could do it perfectly, unlike those people who jump from one task to another.

She described the location of her village as being near a mountain, which sometimes brought forth smoke and at other times fire. This usually indicated that the gods were angry. Apparently, there had been a lot of smoke recently and there was talk that the mountain might soon produce fire, which hadn't happened for many years. The people felt that the gods were displeased with them but did not know why, and the chiefs of the surrounding villages had no answers.

In the past when the mountain produced fire, it was decided the people were not living the way the gods had intended and changes were made. This sometimes involved recognizing people who had committed harmful acts and displeased the gods. The evil ones were described as having very dark hearts, and Kalingah could see the colors surrounding their hearts that identified them. Sometimes they could be helped, but not on every occasion, which meant they had to be "sent away." If someone was very evil, he could be put to death.

The final decision was made by the chief, who would consult the priest and sometimes come to Kalingah and ask her whether the person could be helped. This was a big responsibility for Kalingah but one she accepted as her duty. When asked whether people feared her because of this responsibility, she replied, "No, because I speak the truth."

Neither did they fear the chief, because the people respected him. She said it was hard for her brother Lim, as he had taken on the mantle of chief from their father and then had to earn the villagers' ongoing respect. A big challenge for Lim was that many people did not like one of his wives, a very selfish, greedy woman. His other two wives had given him children, but the unpopular wife did not want children and had somehow discovered how to avoid becoming pregnant.

Kalingah said that although she could create potions to help prevent pregnancy, she had not given any of these to her brother's wife. Tribal laws decreed that if preventing pregnancy went against the wishes of the chief, the woman concerned could be regarded as a troublemaker. Kalingah's father had wanted her brother's wives to produce more grandchildren for him, but now that he was dead, it would be up to the new chief, in this instance the woman's husband, to make the decision. Lim would take advice from the priest, and it was hoped that the wife could be helped and persuaded to change her ways.

An important aspect of life in Kalingah's village was the pursuit of truth and harmony. Life was well ordered in this balanced society, with men and women enjoying equality in many areas. She described how important a peaceful existence was to the villagers, so much so that wrongdoers were sent away if they could not be helped. It was believed that if the people were at peace, then the gods would be at peace with them. The villagers worked hard and enjoyed a simple life in these idyllic surroundings.

At that moment the mountain rumbled and Kalingah once again wondered why the gods were angry. Was there a troublemaker in their village, perhaps her brother's wife, who had upset the gods, or was the problem in one of the surrounding villages? Whatever the reason, Kalingah was frightened of the fire that might engulf them all. She knew her brother's first big test as the new chief would be to appease the gods and so earn the respect of his people.

17

The Wise Woman

Several months later, listening to the recording of my regression, I became enthralled with the story of Kalingah, and on several occasions had to consciously pull myself back to the present day. It is a strange experience to hear yourself describing in such detail a life lived nearly thirteen centuries ago. However, the more I listened to Kalingah tell her story, the prouder I became of leading such a life completely dedicated to the welfare of others. But there was still more to come.

In my next connection with Kalingah she described herself as being much older and had now assumed the mantle of "the wise woman." She looked back on her years of experience and teaching, describing it as a good life. The energy level coming from this older, wiser woman was much quieter and softer than it had been in previous connections, and she described herself as being fairly reclusive at this stage of her life. Kalingah was reticent to talk much about herself—it was obvious to me that the wise woman had no need to extol her own virtues—although she did mention the extensive knowledge she had accumulated over this lifetime. While she also admitted that her life was sometimes lonely, Kalingah revealed she had many dreams in which she connected with her ancestors, so she was able to find comfort in their presence and their wisdom.

When asked, Kalingah recalled the earlier time of the volcano eruption, and said her brother earned the respect of his village when he helped his people. Although many died in other villages, Kalingah said her village was spared because the gods protected them. So her brother was seen as passing the test of the gods and revered by all the tribe. Perhaps his situation was improved when his troublesome third wife died. When asked whether this was from natural causes, Kalingah replied simply, "So it is believed."

Looking back on her life's work as a healer, Kalingah was pleased she had been able to help many people, although she said her abilities were not unique, nor was she special. She was one of several villagers who worked in supporting others. Kalingah described her life as being very happy and satisfying because she was able to give without the need to take from others. As a vital part of her healing work Kalingah enjoyed a strong connection with nature, plants, and animals, which she described as being very special to her. I was shown an image of her sitting quietly on her own, high on a hilltop, watching the sun setting in a crimson blaze, spreading its magnificence across the water. In a state of meditation and prayer, she was connecting with the power of the gods of nature.

As Kalingah was taken forward in her life, she quietly revealed that she had now lived for "more than fifty summers," and her voice grew tired as her energy became weaker. The average lifetime in her village was around forty years, with some living to forty-five, and Kalingah said that she was now feeling very old.

Contact with Kalingah was advanced to the time just before leaving her body. She was resigned to her fate and said she was ready to go now, having no further need of her old body. Kalingah said her head had been hurting for some time and she was not sure why. She was puzzled by this, saying she had tried several mixtures, but none had worked. One of her former students was making her death mask, but she was not allowed to see it, because it was "as others see me." She added that it was also a symbol of how the ancestors regarded her.

Thinking about her life as she lay quietly preparing for death, Kalingah felt a wave of sadness drift over her. She realized that while she was able to open her arms to many people to help them in their healing, she had never fully opened her heart to anyone—she had never given herself completely to another. As her life force started to ebb, Kalingah accepted that while she had been content in her work, this was the one thing that was missing from her lifetime.

When the breath left her pain-racked body for the last time, Kalingah's spirit floated free, looking down on the priest and the young women who were preparing for her funeral. Her voice took on a new energy as she described seeing her death mask for the first time. She was delighted at her mask, confirming for her that the people of her village loved her. She knew then that her life's work had been successful and that the gods were happy with her.

Her brother Lim, the chief of the village, now an old man, stood next to the body as they conducted the funeral ceremony, and while there was sadness in his heart, he knew that it was her time to go. Kalingah, with the wisdom of the free spirit, realized that he, too, would be reaching his time soon.

Kalingah said a little regretfully that she would have liked to have had children to say goodbye to, but she knew her family were those people that she had been able to help through her healing work. She could feel the love of the people for her. There were no tears at her funeral because everyone knew it was her time. In her village there was an understanding that death was part of life, and not to be feared.

Before crossing back into the afterlife, Kalingah's spirit, now free from the restrictions of her physical body, looked back on her life in that simple jungle village. She said the major lesson she had chosen to learn was the power of giving, and also learning to receive love as opposed to material possessions. She had no regrets, although there were some people she would have liked to help a lot more, but it was not to be. Her other lesson was to learn to be alone, without the support of a marriage partner and children. Her lack of physical comforts was compensated for by her spiritual contacts.

Kalingah was now content to wait for the gods to deliver their verdict when she returned to the world of her ancestors.

Everyone has unique gifts and talents. What you love is what you're gifted at. To be completely happy, to live a completely fulfilled life, you have to do what you love.

—BARBARA SHER,
author and counselor[1]

18

Kalingah Returns to the Heaven World

Kalingah's spirit floated gently back across the divide into the world of spirit, where she was met by her father. She knew it was her father, but he looked different from the way she remembered him from his life as the village chieftain. She described him as emanating a male energy, but he now had very pale skin and a beard. A little bewildered, she said, "It is my father, but it's not my father, yet I know it is him."

Her father's spirit explained that she was seeing him in the image of how he would look in his next life. He was showing her that we do not stay the same. He said he could portray himself in whatever way he chose and he wished to take on the appearance of his next life as part of his preparation for it. He wanted to experience the feeling of being that person before he returned to earth. He also told Kalingah that she would not be sharing the next lifetime with him.

Kalingah's father spoke of the preparation for this new life as part of the ongoing nature of the life cycle. He reminded her that each life is but one of many. He confirmed that his guides were helping him in this preparation and also made reference to the ancestors. He was going to be an important man in his next life and was receiving special training in the afterlife for this role. He told Kalingah that he'd had numerous lives in which his decisions affected the lives of many people, and it would be the same in his next incarnation. His destiny was to be an important figure on earth.

He was also able to change his appearance to show her an image of the way he had looked in his previous life. When Kalingah asked about other lives they had shared, her father told her they were together in Roman times as brothers in arms and had many adventures. She was shown an image of them traveling on a road together, both wearing leather helmets and red capes over tunics.

> *The end of life is to be like God, and the soul following God will be like Him.*
>
> —SOCRATES, 469–399 BCE

Her father wanted to welcome Kalingah back to the spirit world as a member of her soul family but also to honor their connection in the previous life. Kalingah described how good it felt to be "home" again and how she was able to enjoy a sense of embracing her father, even though they had no physical bodies. She was able to have an awareness of her own image, which she said no longer looked old, but instead soft.

Kalingah talked proudly about the importance of family relationships for the people in her village. She was happy to have helped them as their healer and wise woman, but now that she was back in the world of spirit, Kalingah was a little shocked to realize how simple the remedies were that she prescribed. Later, Kalingah was able to return to earth in spirit and discovered how much of her healing was done with heart energy. This was achieved not only through the power of intention, but also by putting a lot of love into her healing methods.

Kalingah now also realized that the spiritual messages she received as the wise woman were from the spirits of her ancestors and not from "the gods." "There are no gods the way we saw them," she said. "We thought we were appeasing the gods, but we were really communicating with the spirits of our ancestors who were helping us." She added that the wisdom passed on from the spirits of the ancestors to guide people on earth "has been going on for many, many lifetimes."

Kalingah was also reunited with other members of her soul family, and we discovered that one of her sisters, whom she was very close to, was known to me as Judy. Kalingah's sister died several years before her, and Kalingah was able to put all her love into her sister's death mask. There were very strong family ties between them and Kalingah loved her sister and her sister's children deeply. In particular,

Kalingah enjoyed a close bond with one of her nieces, whom she had trained as a healer and whose spirit has incarnated as my daughter Rebecca.

My guide M later confirmed that Rebecca and I have experienced several lifetimes together, as my mother in one life and as my son in another. We all tend to reincarnate in soul groups in a variety of relationships to help one another learn and grow spiritually, so this was not surprising to me. However, I'm not sure how my daughter will take the news of having played mother to me in the past.

The deep but unexplainable familiarity we have with certain people in our current life can often be traced to past-life connections. It is comforting to know that when someone very close to us passes over, it is never the end, just a new beginning. We will see them again and very possibly enjoy many earthly experiences in a future incarnation.

19

Soul Energy Guidance

When we reincarnate, we always leave a certain portion of our soul energy in the afterlife that is able to work independently to the soul attached to our body. This is sometimes referred to as our higher self, or oversoul, and is able to access information from other incarnations as well as oversee our current life. More details on this are given in chapter 38. In the regression, Colleen was able to communicate directly with my soul energy, seeking to receive details of my past lives.

My past-life regression with Colleen took place just before Christmas, and I decided to take a break for the holidays and not listen to the recording of the session until after the festive season. So it wasn't until several weeks later that I played the recording for the first time. It was the strangest feeling—hearing another part of me speaking about my soul's progress through several lifetimes in a detached, straightforward, and honest way. It almost felt as if I were not in the room at the time.

My soul energy confirmed that I'd had many other lives as a healer, with a very significant one as a priest in ancient Egypt. This lifetime was spent in the Temple of Isis, but it was a more ceremonial role rather than any involving direct healing practices. Even though I was not asked to go deeper into this lifetime during the session, I readily accepted this information, as I have always been fascinated by the history and culture of ancient Egypt. I have visited many ancient sites there—some more than once—and also collected many Egyptian artifacts and books, including statues and carved images of the gods. And of course my romantic adventures with Carol took place in the land of the pharaohs.

When asked what I needed to learn from these past-life experiences, my soul energy said that I basically needed to know I have led lives where I was able to help people. My most recent past life, when I was killed in the Great War, was the culmination of many lives as a soldier. It took numerous lifetimes to achieve this completion. In my current life I need to understand that even though I've been destructive in the past, I have also helped people, and it is very important to achieve a balance in our life cycles.

It also bore out John Dingwall's words, that spiritual growth is achieved through many lifetimes, and we often take our karma from one life to the next to resolve major issues. We can develop wonderful qualities in one lifetime, such as displayed by Kalingah, but still have other unresolved blockages that need to be addressed in another.

As I listened to the recording, I was encouraged to hear that I can help people in this lifetime, though in a way different from Kalingah's. The message was not to feel guilty about being a soldier, and now that one side of my progression had been completed in Kalingah's life as a physical healer, I needed to bring a different aspect into focus.

There are many forms of healing, and one does not necessarily need to practice as a doctor, a counselor, or even a spiritual healer to accomplish this. My soul energy identified my accumulated knowledge, the ability to communicate, and the use of spiritual and intuitive abilities as the keys to my healing activities in this life. This has been evidenced by my intuitive readings as well as my books. My soul energy also confirmed that I have the ability to bring in the combined knowledge and experience of these two previous lifetimes as Kalingah and the Egyptian priest.

I listened to my soul speak to me directly and dispassionately, beyond the normal emotions I am caught up in each day. As I thought about this later, it occurred to me that my regression to my life as Kalingah the healer was, in fact, drawn from the memories stored in my subconscious mind. I had a strong sense that further material would be available to me through deep meditation now that the door had been opened to my distant past.

Our soul energy is able to access any of our past lives when it decides regression to a particular incarnation is appropriate for our growth. It doesn't matter whether we are here on earth or back in the afterlife, accessing the Akashic Records. I realized how valuable it was to explore my past-life recall in detail, to glean the many insights it offered to light the way in this lifetime.

Looking back objectively on Kalingah's life, I could see that she achieved a lot of positive things. She was a selfless and effective healer who gave up any thoughts of marriage and children, no matter how challenging that was, to dedicate her life to the welfare of the community. It demonstrates that we do not always need earthly trappings to lead a happy and successful life. After getting to know and understand Kalingah, I believe that my soul growth from that lifetime was enormous.

20

The Wisdom of M

When I listened to the recording of my past-life regression, much of the information came as a complete surprise, although I was able to recall sketchy aspects of my life as Kalingah when I came out of the hypnotic state. But the biggest shock came when I heard Colleen ask me to connect with my guide and then requested details about him. I had never talked to her about my guide M, and she had not read *Afterlife*, so this question was unexpected. However, I realized there had to be a reason for the query, otherwise my guide M would not have permitted the contact. M only provides guidance for my writing and not my personal life, and has always been reticent about coming forward. He prefers to remain in the background, inspiring me with his gentle, loving presence.

I am very grateful for M's presence, as he is with me every step of the way, feeding me thoughts, helping form ideas, and confirming or rejecting information that I receive from my many sources. I treasure that part of M that inspires my writing.

During the regression my soul energy immediately tuned in that it was indeed M whom Colleen was asking about, and not another guide. M allowed me to tell her that he has traveled far as a soul and has had many significant earthly lives. I was honored to learn that I had been with him in a past life in England, around the turbulent time of the Reformation. King Henry VIII was on the throne and in addition to collecting six wives, he was responsible for the creation of the Church of England. This entailed the destruction and looting of many Catholic churches and also mass killings under the direction of Thomas Cromwell. The turmoil then continued during the reign of his daughter Queen Elizabeth I.

As I listened back to this information from M, I was delighted, as I had no conscious memory of this contact. The remarkable thing was that during my Christmas holiday break I had been focusing a lot of my thoughts and interest on Tudor times, which turned out to be the very period in history when we were together on earth. M revealed that he had been a very high-ranking authority figure in those times, and I was one of his assistants.

It was a turbulent era when there was a great power struggle for the hearts and minds of the people as the Roman Catholic Church and the monarchy vied for control. At such dark and troubled times there are always great souls who hold the light of reason, justice, and compassion while still remaining solid. I believe M was such a person.

M has been a master guide for a long time. As a master guide he is easily able to split his spiritual energy to be in various places at once, and chooses to incarnate when it is necessary. While he may agree to play an important role in history, it would not be for self-aggrandizement. Obviously deciding he didn't want to become the focus of attention in the regression, M firmly moved the direction of the questions away from him and back to me.

I later communicated directly with M and got his permission to include this information. He would not tell me, even off the record, which important figure he was in that lifetime, nor indeed who I was. He would confirm only that it was during the reign of Queen Elizabeth I. Pushing my luck, I cheekily asked him whether he was, in fact, the swashbuckling Sir Francis Drake, which he laughingly denied.

> *From the moment of conception, and even before that, there*
> *is attached to the incarnating soul someone who volunteers*
> *to be his guardian.*
>
> —SILVER BIRCH'

21

The Connections Continue

The surprise of connecting with M during the regression was followed by another revelation that opened my heart and answered many questions for me about my current life.

When Kalingah's spirit returned to the afterlife and was welcomed home by her father, my current partner, Anne, was also there. That's when I fully realized the strength of the soul connection between Anne and me. I saw that in the afterlife, Anne's spirit and mine were very close. We enjoyed many recreational activities together, and also supported each other individually and in group situations as we prepared for our next incarnation.

A later consultation with medium Ruth Phillips revealed other pieces of the jigsaw. I discovered that Anne and I have shared many past lives and relationships, encompassing everything from brothers in arms to lovers. We were often part of the same family, even sisters in one life. Before this incarnation, it was decided that our souls would benefit most if we connected at a later stage in life.

That didn't mean to say there weren't issues to face. At first Anne and I experienced difficulties in our current relationship, mainly because I was still grieving over the loss of Judy. But these issues were necessary for us both, as part of our development. My late partner Judy was a great organizer, so it came as no surprise to hear that her spirit had been instrumental in Anne and me meeting again.

Deep down I knew that I had been completing several karmic relationships in this lifetime, something that Ruth confirmed. One of my missions in this incarnation is to learn *a lot* about relationships: romantic, family, in the workplace, and many more. Part of the reason Anne is in my life is to help me round off these lessons with her love and strong support.

I was recovering from the loss of Judy when Anne and I first met at a spiritual festival. We soon discovered that we lived only a few blocks away from each other on the outskirts of the city. This was a delightful piece of synchronicity, and I took the opportunity of inviting Anne to be one of my first guests on *Radio Out There*, which was starting that week on live radio. When I discovered she wasn't in a relationship, I invited her out and we went to the theater. We soon realized we had a lot in common and really enjoyed each other's company. In those early days of our friendship Anne helped me move through the emotional fog of my grief to embrace a new future. As things progressed, we connected at a deep level. When I look at our relationship now I realize it reflects the love and the intimacy we share as soul companions in the Heaven World.

For it was not into my ear you whispered, but into my heart.
It was not my lips you kissed, but my soul.

—JUDY GARLAND, 1922–1969

As well as our shared spiritual interests, Anne has awakened in me a love of art galleries, particularly in Paris! We are both passionate about travel, and the world regularly beckons us. Anne constantly challenges and encourages me to grow and learn in every possible way. Most important, I have found love with a warm and beautiful soul companion when I thought I would never be truly happy again after Judy's death.

As for the role I play in Anne's life, you'll have to ask her!

22

The Council of Elders

Many people fear death because they believe they will be judged for what they have done in their lives and then punished accordingly. We all have to face up to the deeds we've committed in our life when we return to the afterlife, but there is no stern figure sitting on a throne dishing out thunderbolts and one-way directions to some cosmic naughty corner.

Instead we meet with a Council of Elders who have been observing us, possibly over many lifetimes, and helping us evolve as souls. Far from meting out punishment, the Elders help us in a life review to realize what we have achieved and where we have deviated from our path. The look back on our previous life is done in a loving and positive way, but we do get to experience directly the hurt we have caused others so that we can empathize with their pain.

After Kalingah had been welcomed back into the world of spirit by her father, she experienced a brief period of healing, in which, she said, she felt as if many hands were placed on her spiritual being. Now reenergized, Kalingah knew she would soon face the Council of Elders, or ancestors, as she referred to them. She had a very humble attitude to this meeting. "They know when they are ready that I am ready," was her simple acceptance of the situation.

The most remarkable thing then happened in the regression. My guidance revealed that the Elders had also given their blessing for my current spiritual energy to be present as an observer when Kalingah's spirit met them for her life review. This is a perfect example of how linear time does not exist in the spirit world.

The way the Council of Elders appears to a spirit differs with each person. Some spirits see them sitting formally in a big hall or other majestic setting. For others, they may be in very informal surroundings. As I watched from the sidelines, Kalingah found herself in the kind of hut that would be appropriate to a village chief. She was full of respect for that setting, as she was still coming to terms with being back in the afterlife.

The Council of Elders welcomed Kalingah home, and she felt reassured and more comfortable, because it had been very easy for her to believe that she was being put on trial in this meeting. The Council recognized that Kalingah believed, through her upbringing, that spirits were strongly judged on what they had done in their life and that any wrongdoing would be punished in the afterlife. So the Elders assured her that this was not the case, and there was no judgment. There might be special education or training to undergo, but no punishment.

Kalingah had a male and three female-type energies around her as she met with the Council. All the Elders addressed her at various times and no one seemed to be in charge. They were pleased with her life's work as a healer, which had atoned in some way for several of her past incarnations as a warrior in which she had taken others' lives. The Council told her that she had earned a period of respite after giving so much in her previous life. She could now just "rest and be," and when she was ready they would call her and offer her a suitable life in another incarnation.

At this time the earth's population was very small, so opportunities for a new life were limited and spirits spent longer periods in the afterlife. Spirits had to wait until another body was ready for them and the offer of the right body in appropriate life circumstances was decided by the Council. It was made clear to me as I observed the Elders that just to have a body, a life, was of no significance, as our time on earth is about learning and growth for our soul needs. But it is not just on earth where we can learn and grow. There is much learning that can happen in spirit and on other worlds. Earthly incarnations are just part of a larger opportunity for growth, and we keep returning until we have had every experience we need.

Kalingah was happy to know the Elders were very pleased with the way she had led her life. They made it clear that she had gotten over a major hurdle in her development by helping others. They emphasized this one was in stark contrast to those past lives as a warrior, which had been more focused on violence and selfishly taking what she wanted from people. Kalingah described her earthly life as a long one in relation to the number of years other people lived in those times. Not surprisingly, she was still very weary after so many years of service, so the Elders granted her a long rest in the afterlife before her next incarnation.

Her earthly body was worn out, so her spirit needed more healing as well as rest before the next stage of her journey. The Elders told her there were many things for her to explore and learn in the world of spirit before she needed to return to earth. Rest is essential in the afterlife, as it not only restores a spirit's strength but also lets us work with our guides to learn more about ourselves.

It was interesting to observe how Kalingah's energy lifted noticeably as she realized she would have the opportunity to enjoy herself now that she had returned to pure spirit form. This was a big change from her life on earth, which was mainly confined to work. Now she would be completely free to enjoy being in nature, and be with friends and family. She asked if she could assist those who had just returned to the afterlife, as these spirits could be very confused and still hurting from their life experiences, and was later given permission to do so.

Everybody in the afterlife is expected to help others in some way, so Kalingah's request to become a healer in spirit was not surprising. "While spirits don't have a body, what they bring over into our world still needs healing," Kalingah explained.

This was an interesting insight, as people cross over with many things still in their minds, and even though they have left their physical form behind, they can feel as if they still have a body with all its problems and ailments. This is similar to when some people who have had an arm or a leg amputated retain the sensation that it is still there; it is often referred to as a phantom limb. Kalingah revealed she would start this work once her own healing was complete.

Kalingah spoke of particularly wanting to help other people who cross over with mental problems. She said that not everything can be fixed in the afterlife, because it may be part of their karma. Interestingly, in one of our sessions conducted several months later, John's group also had some thought-provoking things to say about mental problems.

According to Kalingah, certain ailments of the heart or mind stay with a spirit and become part of its next incarnation. Sometimes people need to go back to earth to face the same experiences again so that they can work out the answers themselves. Kalingah emphasized there is a lot of help offered to us in the spirit world, but it ultimately comes down to our taking responsibility for the things we do. She said, "We are not judged, but we have to answer to our ancestors and to ourselves as to why we do these things."

You may never know what results come from your action.
But if you do nothing, there will be no result.

—MOHANDAS K. GANDHI, 1869–1948

By this time Kalingah had rejoined her soul family, those people with whom she had been bound together in spirit over the ages. We are all part of a soul family, which is our ultimate support group. We often reincarnate with members of this family, and they can play various roles in our life, from lovers and family to friends and even adversaries. Often we do not encounter other members of our soul family in our earthly existence, as they may be off exploring other opportunities, or they could still be in spirit. However, we do communicate on many occasions in the dream state when our spirit leaves our body and connects with other spirits and guides.

Kalingah soon realized that she was the only healer in her soul group, and the others had different duties. However, when they all got together, they talked about family matters and helped one another, much the way many families do on earth. They were still able to be together as a family in the afterlife, even though their individual growth was at different stages. Kalingah compared this to a family on earth, of which some members might have important positions while others were still learning, but they were all part of a family unit.

When she had completed her initial healing, Kalingah still had a strong need for rest, but was unsure of what to do. She asked her guide, "Where do I go, where do I rest my head, do I just lie under a tree?" She wondered whether she would have her own hut, the way she had in the jungle village. Her guide told her that she could create whatever resting place she chose, because in spirit a person is restricted only by the imagination.

Yet despite this vastness of choice, Kalingah still yearned for the simplicity of her jungle hut, feeling the need for the familiarity of the forest and her earthly surroundings she loved so much.

After her meeting with the Council, Kalingah was able to rest and enjoy recreations such as walking, listening to music, and being with other spirits. She could enjoy the full freedom of the spirit world, unlike the restrictions surrounding her last life. Here, there was everything she could wish for. She was able to visit old friends and eventually start work again as a healer, something that gave her a great sense of satisfaction.

When she was ready, she would also be able to accompany her guide to the Hall of Akashic Records, where she could access her previous lives. Having access to previous lives can be very illuminating, but it is not just for fun. Spirits have to know why they are going to look at and experience their other lives before being given permission to investigate. This helps them understand where they are now, what they've learned, and how they've progressed. It's a truly amazing opportunity.

23

Helping Our Earth Family

You don't choose your family. They are God's gift to you, as you are to them.

—DESMOND TUTU

One of the great concerns for those people facing death is the prospect of leaving their loved ones behind when they pass over. For grief-stricken families, the thought of never seeing someone again after they die is distressing.

The good news is that our loved ones are still able to contact us from the other side, and that spirits also get to spend time with us on a regular basis. There are enough genuine mediums in the world providing evidence of survival in the afterlife to prove this. Just prior to my finishing this book, Anne and I attended the Arthur Findlay College in the UK, recognized as the preeminent training center in the Western world for mediums. We were privileged to work with some of Britain's most talented mediums as they conducted a weeklong residential course. For me, it was like a postgraduate course. Not only did it enhance my own skills as a medium, I was also able to witness first-hand the benefits of contacting the spirit world by some of the best mediums on the planet.

When we are able to communicate with someone who has physically disappeared from our life and listen to their story, it removes both fear and doubt about our ongoing life as a soul. You only have to look at the faces of people who have received a message from a spirit to see the positive impact it has.

Kalingah was given permission by the ancestors to return to earth as a spirit to help her family and friends. She was not able to interfere in their lives, but simply being with them and providing love and support were more than enough for her. Sometimes she was able to whisper quietly in their ear or visit them in their dreams to offer help and advice.

Even when people ask for help from family or friends in spirit, it is not always possible—or even allowed—for spirits to provide all the answers they are seeking. Kalingah soon discovered that people cannot be given help from spirit just because they ask; there are many occasions when they must make choices themselves. Permission must be also obtained for spirits to work with people at any stage of their life; they cannot simply decide to slip down to earth and take action themselves. In addition to help from family and friends in spirit, support is also available from guides, teachers, and Elders when the situation is appropriate. Kalingah added, "There are many people in the afterlife who help those on earth."

She went on to say that it is far easier for spirits to connect with people in the dream state, and permission does not always have to be sought for these meetings, because the person's spirit has left the body at this time. These meetings can be of great assistance in our decision-making process, without actually influencing that decision inappropriately. This, however, does not mean that all dreams have a message, according to Kalingah. Some dreams give us help, some have a message, and some connect us with our loved ones. She added, in some dreams, "It may just be our mind."

Kalingah confirmed that we can all return to the world of spirit in the dream state and connect with our soul family. We are also able to communicate with our guides in times of great stress, but we don't always completely remember this exchange. Sometimes people wake up the next morning not necessarily recollecting their dream, just *knowing* what they have to do.

Kalingah emphasized that not only was she forbidden from interfering in any way in people's lives, but she must also respect their privacy. This is a very important point. Many people express concern about spirits being present at very personal times in their life. The very thought of one of our dear departed parents, an aunt, or a grandmother dropping in or hanging around when we are enjoying intimate moments, for example, is enough to make anyone run scream-ing from the house.

Anyone who senses the unwanted presence of spirits around their house can ask their guide for assistance, or simply ask the spirit to leave. Guides will often arrange for spirits who have not crossed over to be helped to do so. If the problem persists, specialized help, such as a medium, may be needed.

24

Kalingah's Next Life

As this long and involved regression continued, we moved forward in Kalingah's sojourn in the afterlife to the point where she was preparing for her next incarnation. This new lifetime would take Kalingah into a completely opposing environment, and would provide a very different set of circumstances for her projected experiences.

The Council of Elders had offered Kalingah's spirit a life as a trader in a desert region, which was in stark contrast to the jungles of Central America. This time her soul would be given the body of a man, whose father was a desert nomad, in what is now known as the Middle East. My guide M later confirmed it was in a region we know as Syria, in the early part of the twelfth century, just after the First Crusade.

The purpose of this lifetime would be to interact with a diverse group of people, and the main lesson would be to understand the range of emotions and experiences that such a mix of societies can provide. As a man in this life Kalingah would also have to come to terms with the fact that this would not be the gentle, peaceful life she enjoyed in her previous incarnation.

During this next incarnation there would be experiences involving turbulence, greed, and materialism, which would be the complete opposite of those in Kalingah's life. However, this is the whole point of each incarnation; once we have reached a certain point in our learning, there is no use in going back over old ground, no matter how much we may yearn for the past. Kalingah summed it up succinctly: "We have different lives to experience all that there is, with many temptations and choices placed in front of us."

As a young boy in the next life, Kalingah's spirit would also face widespread cruelty, which would allow him to see how others live in such a harsh environment. He would discover that inhumanity is part of humanity, and that all is not peace and love. But he would have the opportunity to bring in the love and peacefulness that he had achieved in his past life as Kalingah to cope with these challenging emotions.

During his time on earth he would be living in a brutal world, but would have opportunities to improve his life and help others, from the wisdom contained within his soul. He would be placed in a position to understand why people would want to live in this unforgiving manner and, most important, to realize that situations change as we all are offered many choices and opportunities in life.

Kalingah's spirit spent many years of earth time preparing for what she realized was to be a grueling experience in several ways. In the afterlife, much of this planning was done in a group situation, where she had to face various options and role-play potential scenarios, which were then buried deep within the boy's subconscious mind for his benefit in the life to come. Her father's spirit had long since reincarnated, but she was able to work with her brother Lim, the former village chief now back in spirit, who was a member of her soul family. In this new life, however, she would not have direct contact with any of her soul family and would have to undergo this strict test on her own. This life would be an important part of her development and as such more demanding than previous experiences.

Whether this young man chose to listen to his inner voice or give in to temptation would be up to him, and would be the whole point of the test. At vulnerable times like this during our lives we need to pause, think, and listen to that inner wisdom and not make rushed decisions. This is where our deep sense of knowing the best action for our highest benefit comes from.

His guides would also be whispering in his ear, along with other spirit helpers, but greed for material possessions would be a huge temptation placed in front of him. This would be an arduous life, but Kalingah's spirit had a long period of rest to prepare for it. There would be many lessons to learn, which may or may not be resolved by the end of this lifetime, potentially creating karmic debt that would have to be carried forward into other incarnations.

Fortunately, he would be traveling with some supporting members of adjoining soul groups and would be helped by them at various times. At times he would experience what he would regard as a strange series of events, but would discover that everything has a reason. Quite often, members of our soul family and our support groups incarnate before us and manifest as parents, friends, colleagues, and even enemies, to work with us. Sometimes our worst enemy can be a soul supporter playing out a pre-arranged role for our mutual benefit. Naturally we perform the same functions for other people as well. Life contracts often can be very complex, as we will discuss later.

Unexpected situations that arise can create a very challenging time in our lives, and even though we may have rehearsed our options in spirit, one decision—good or bad—can affect the lives of many people. It can also create karmic issues that take several lifetimes to work through.

> *Better to live in a desert than with a quarrelsome and*
> *ill-tempered wife.*
>
> —PROVERBS 21:19

Kalingah's spirit was soon to discover the truth of that quote from the Bible.

25

The Lessons Continue

Mistakes are the portals of discovery.

—JAMES JOYCE, 1882–1941,
author of *Ulysses*

The knowledge I gained from my regression to Kalingah's life was overwhelming, and I had much to be grateful for. But my soul energy had a final gift for me—the opportunity to look back and examine the lessons of my next life as a twelfth-century desert trader.

The boy was given the name Arloon. He was born into a Middle Eastern country, and living conditions in these times were described as very harsh. Slavery was accepted as a way of life, but Arloon's father was not wealthy enough to trade in slaves, so instead he ran a successful enterprise dealing in "trinkets and whatever he could."

Arloon described his father as being essentially a kind man, but he possessed a cruel streak, which apparently was a common trait among people at that time, and had inherited it from his own father. Arloon, too, had this potential for cruelty as part of his genetic makeup, but by exercising his free will he was able to contain this aspect of his background to a great extent as he proceeded through life.

Arloon went on to achieve far more success as a trader than his father did, and although he did not trade in slaves, there were several slaves in his household staff. There was no evil intent in keeping people as slaves, it was "just the way things were in that society." In fact, Arloon saw it as his right. Unfortunately, every now and then, his inherited cruel streak emerged in the way he treated his slaves as well as other people in his family, such as on those occasions when he wanted to get his own way.

To become a successful trader, he learned to be very cunning, so that others would not take advantage of him. Arloon and his family lived in a town that has long since disappeared from the map, but he frequently visited the city of Damascus on his trading ventures. It was here he gave in to the delights and temptations that a big city offered to someone from a small town with money in his purse.

Before long the accumulation of wealth and possessions became all-important, and this included being able to purchase his personal slaves and bodyguards. Arloon collected and displayed fine carpets and other possessions in his home so that he could flaunt his wealth and importance to others. He had a big ego and gave in easily to all kinds of enticements that were conveniently placed in his path. My soul energy described Arloon as "not a bad man, but just someone of his times in many ways." Survival was a strong focus for him, along with the driving force to be better than other people.

Arloon eventually died in his mid-forties, in the same desert in which he was born. He was on a trading mission when he was caught in a wild sandstorm, which wiped out his entire caravan.

When Arloon returned to the afterlife, he received a very different reaction to that of his life as Kalingah. The Elders, of course, knew all about the temptations he faced, and in his life review they let him experience for himself how other people were affected by some of these choices. Arloon was made to feel their pain and frustrations and was shown how he could have made better choices in life. Feeling ashamed and disappointed with himself, he went back to his soul family, with whom these and other choices were analyzed and discussed in great detail to help everyone in the group in their future lives. Life reviews are not courts of judgment, and often we are our own harshest critic when we remember what we set out to achieve in that lifetime.

Although Arloon didn't intentionally hurt his slaves, the Elders felt that subconsciously he knew it was inappropriate behavior, because of his previous life as Kalingah and also his intense spiritual preparation in the afterlife. Arloon could have chosen a simpler lifestyle whereby he did not buy slaves or enjoy other temptations, but instead he gave in to his ego. He knew deep down in his soul that this was against his spiritual values, but he allowed himself to be driven by outer circumstances and made poor choices, profiting by others' misery.

Arloon realized that his was a life dominated by ego and greed, in which he seemed to ignore basic family values for his own selfish indulgences. Arloon had a long-suffering but argumentative wife who bore him four sons, and he also purchased several concubines for his pleasure. Although the keeping of concubines was an accepted part of his society, sadly Arloon favored them over his wife and family.

Looking back on this life as Arloon the desert trader, my soul energy said that his lifestyle reflects the choices many people make in the twenty-first century. It is easy to get swept along by the current of our environment and the social conditions of the day, but it is important that we dig deep within ourselves and listen to our inner knowing. Our past-life memories have been submerged at birth to avoid confusion, but are still found in our soul memory. It is important that we make a conscious choice to look inside ourselves before making major decisions.

My soul energy said that the information in our subconscious mind has been programmed during our time in the world of spirit. Some people call this their conscience. It is available to us all if we make the effort to listen.

The Elders told Arloon that he would not have another life on earth for a long time. There would be ample opportunity to reassess the life just completed, and learn every lesson that was possible from his actions. There was no point in having a cursory examination and then putting his life just lived to one side and asking for another body to be available. There were many issues that needed intense exploration in a life that was self-serving with little thought for others. In his group work Arloon examined the positive choices that he could have made, and how they would have worked out for him and his retinue.

This was a life completely opposite to that of Kalingah, and Arloon realized several future lifetimes would now be necessary to work out the karmic issues he created. If we don't learn from our past mistakes, we have to keep coming back to earth until we do, and until our karma is balanced.

When asked about the human belief in the difference between right and wrong as evidenced by these two lives, the answer I received from my soul energy was simple and direct: "There is no right and there is no wrong; it is the experience of how it affects us and how it touches others. There is no judgment in the afterlife; right and wrong are purely human terms."

The hardest lesson of all is for us to use our intuition and access the wisdom from these group sessions that have been implanted in our subconscious in the afterlife. As we go through each lifetime, we are far more likely to react to our challenging surroundings and situations without thinking, let alone using our intuition or meditating. So we have to keep returning to earth to learn how to listen to our inner wisdom, and react to many different situations in the interests of everyone's highest benefit in our life.

Part Three

New Directions

26

Soul Growth

Whatever your trials, remind yourself that you are a spirit
and are capable of changing your destiny.

—OMRAAM MIKHAËL AÏVANHOV, 1900–1986,
Macedonian philosopher, mystic, and alchemist

We all have hardships that we have to face in each lifetime, no matter who we are or how advanced is our soul. In fact, "old souls" are often those burdened the most with many lifetimes of karma to work through. We are unlikely to advance if we breeze through life without a worry or a care.

Knowing that the next life was going to be very arduous, Kalingah's spirit could have refused if she chose. Not everything is set in stone. In most cases the Elders do give us choices before we accept a life contract. Some spirits do not want to reincarnate under any circumstances, particularly after a difficult life, and may be allowed to stay for long periods in the afterlife. Other reluctant spirits are shown compelling reasons why the life being proposed will benefit their development and are encouraged to accept.

If the Council of Elders offers someone a life in which the soul can have growth experiences, subtle pressure and karma can come into play, and in the end there may be no choice but to accept. Spirits are given every help in pre-life preparation with their soul groups, so that they can reincarnate and potentially have those experiences in a positive way. The long-term goal is for each soul to complete a full range of experiences, after which there will eventually be no need to go back to earth.

However, this does not necessarily mean that once the earthly life cycle has ended we can automatically just settle in to an easy life in the spirit world forever. Some souls do reach the point at which they are advanced enough to become teachers and guides, while others are encouraged to explore other worlds for their development. Earth is one of the lower-based planets in our universe, with a very dense energy level. The vibrations are low and very thick, but the learning potential is intense. Life on other inhabited worlds is beyond my subconscious knowledge, as I have yet to experience these domains firsthand. But they are certainly out there, despite wide skepticism, and I look forward to exploring them at some stage.

27

Animals in the Afterlife

A few months before moving to my present location, my beloved black cat, Apollo, left my life. I was working downstairs in my office when some inner alarm bell rang and a message in my head told me to go upstairs and open the front door, even though nobody had knocked. There on the doormat was Apollo, stretched out and unconscious. I knew intuitively that he had been hit by a car, and I rushed him to the vet, tearfully asking God, my guides, or anyone else listening at the time to save him. It was not to be.

My good friend Trisha McCagh, an animal whisperer and medium, had been helping discourage Apollo from bringing dead rodents and other wildlife into the house as a demonstration of his hunting skills.

When I told Trish about Apollo's accident, she volunteered to contact him in the afterlife. Apollo told her it was his time, but he wanted me to be the one who found him because he was my special friend. He had some other personal messages for me so that I would know that it was indeed Apollo's spirit giving the message.

One of the questions often raised whenever I give talks or workshops about the afterlife is about the animals that share our daily lives. People are anxious to know whether they, too, go to the afterlife and are waiting for us when we cross over, or if they disappear into some mysterious place of their own. Some people are even in doubt whether animals have souls. The other point of controversy is whether animals can reincarnate, perhaps even coming back as human beings.

John Dingwall and the team of spirits were most emphatic in their answer about the reincarnation question. Animal and human souls are different. The energy that has been part of an animal cannot normally become a person's. However, it is possible for an advanced being to reincarnate as an animal for an extraordinary purpose, but John added, "Generally that is not done, as they [the spirits] are two different vibrations."

As for meeting up with our cherished animal friends when we return to the afterlife, John said that animals are everywhere, running around freely as part of the spirit community. Animals also have their own special area in the afterlife, but they are encouraged to mingle with the general community of spirits as well. Once we cross over, we are able to reconnect with what John describes as "their familiar vibration." In many cases, beloved animal friends are among the first to meet and greet returning spirits. Their relationship with us then continues in the afterlife.

There are many animal communicators on earth, some referred to as horse whisperers and the like, as well as mediums who are apparently able to connect with animal spirits in the afterlife. Sometimes the messages that come through from animal spirits are very simple. I must admit the funny side of that struck me as I visualized a medium saying *woof* or perhaps *meow* as a message from an animal spirit to a bemused client. But John smartly pulled me back to reality by saying that at other times some very complex information is communicated via the medium. He described this talent as the special ability to tap into a slightly different wavelength.

This contact is often a very special part of a soul's progression. The spirit of that much-loved animal, John said, is strong enough to "push their energy back across to connect with a person on earth, in a similar way to how human energy communicates from the afterlife." It is often an important part of the person's grieving process, as well as soul evolution, to make this connection.

Today more than ever before life must be characterized by a sense of Universal Responsibility, not only nation to nation and human to human, but also human to other forms of life.

—HIS HOLINESS, THE DALAI LAMA

John went on to say that connecting with an animal may be the only way some people can open their hearts. Animal spirits often come back to spend a lot of time with their former human friends, particularly those people who are on their own and very lonely. They share their energy with their human friend and, along with that person's guides and spirit helpers, have their unique role to play in healing.

Sometimes young children will see the spirit of an animal that was part of their family, even though that animal died before they were born. Unfortunately these sightings are usually dismissed under the "imaginary friend" banner.

John, however, disagreed with those people who say that animals can offer us wisdom or guidance from the afterlife. He said animals are capable of passing through their emotions, but guidance is a different matter. His explanation was that there is insufficient vibration for the animal to pass on guidance.

When I asked him about the messages that some mediums receive from animals, John's reply made a lot of sense. "Are those messages really being received from animals?" The information may appear to be coming from animals, but spirits are there as well, overseeing the communication. It is all part of the grieving experience. Higher beings in spirit are also capable of bringing their energy through in the form of an animal. The main thing is that people receive the appropriate information, from whatever source is best for them. Animals in the afterlife are apparently also capable of connecting with spirit energy if they wish to communicate or be with their previous earth friend.

I have sensed Apollo's presence around me several times since his passing, which has helped me cope with his absence from my life. It is also very comforting to know that our animal friends will be waiting when we cross over into the afterlife.

28

Looking into the Future

John's earlier reference to advanced spirits being able to look into the future on earth gave me a lot to think about in the weeks leading up to our next session. So far we had talked about the combination of destiny and free will as part of our life cycles and also the life contract that we all enter into before reincarnating. But John also mentioned that certain events can and do get out of control and build a momentum that is virtually unstoppable. The two world wars of the twentieth century are prime examples. So, revisiting this topic, I asked how far spirits can look into our future from the afterlife, and how much is set in stone.

John confirmed that people on earth have the capability to look ahead, but most people do not use it. Psychics and clairvoyants have learned how to use their ability to a certain extent, but in the spirit world this talent is magnified. In the afterlife this skill varies according to each individual spirit's level of soul growth, so not everyone is able to clearly see into the future. John is not absolutely sure of his own limitations, but sometimes when he asks a question he sees a little screen showing future events. "But I only see what I am allowed to see," he added, admitting that he didn't know what was hidden from him, either.

John described these visions of future events as the "strongest path that will take place." Many factors can change the outcome if the soul (or souls) in question decides to exercise free will and go down entirely different paths. Influences such as drugs and alcohol can also come into play. Individual behavior trends, however, are taken into account by the spiritual planners when looking at probable future paths. A stable person may have a 90 percent chance of staying on the chosen path, whereas an erratic individual's future is hard to plot. It can even mean that a predestined life path can be cut short by extreme behavior.

On a grander scale, John said, some world events appear inevitable, especially those in which several powerful countries are all heading in the same direction. In the early part of the new century, these countries are tearing themselves apart, posing a danger for those nations around them. There are grave concerns in the spirit world over the possibility of "a bloody religious war" at some future point. It is up to the people of the world to give their leaders a strong message that they want peace, not war. Once it gets to a point where there is no going back, even if certain world powers want to withdraw, it will be too late.

John described the situation between very different cultures as "deep-rooted and built out of mistrust." As for the possibility of eternal world peace and a predicted new golden era, John said it will be unlikely in his current sojourn in the afterlife.

As he now resides in a timeless land, who knows how long that may be?

29

Visit from an Old Friend

Chris Kelly was a very talented medium and shamanic healer who helped me prepare for dialogue with the world of spirit when I was researching *Afterlife*. Shamanic healing is an ancient practice that deals with the spiritual aspect of illness. Chris also played a key role in connecting me with the Brazilian healer John of God, from whom I received two amazing crystals that have opened a portal into the vast world of spirit. Chris passed over in a tragic accident on his farm property before my first book was finished, otherwise I believe he would have contributed much more to my research. While in the dream state, I had a brief contact with him about six months after he passed over, but then nothing for a couple of years.

Imagine my delight when Chris unexpectedly made contact with us through Kelly Dale while he was in a trance communicating with John's spirit group. Up until then, the only spirit contact we'd had in these sessions was with the spirit of Kelly's late father, John Dingwall, representing his anonymous support team. This was a breakthrough for Chris, who we discovered had been in the wings with John's group since his passing several years prior, and he was almost beside himself with excitement (that's if a spirit can actually be beside himself!).

When he finally came through from spirit, his opening words were typically Chris: "I'm so ripped to be here!" Chris confirmed that this was the first time he had been able to come through in a trance session, where his spirit was able to enter and embrace the physical body of Kelly to communicate with us. Prior to this he, had been able to pass on several messages through mental mediums and contribute as part of the support group, but that was all. Chris chuckled loudly when he made the breakthrough, gleefully telling us that we didn't know how much it meant to him to make contact like this, "to be able to speak again." He was so excited, he didn't know quite where to start, which was so unlike Chris in his previous life, a man quietly spoken but never at a loss for words. Now he was displaying a new energy level in his enthusiasm to connect with us.

Chris described his situation up to that point as like being in a coma, not being able to pass the information across the divide. "It's like being trapped in a body with everyone looking at you and you are not able to speak or anything else," he said. He repeatedly broke off in midsentence with delighted peals of laughter at his newfound abilities. Chris was like the proverbial kid playing with a new toy.

Since his arrival back in the afterlife, Chris told us, he had visited a lot of places and had been with some "amazing spirits and souls, and also orbs of light." He had also been spending a lot of his time back with loved ones on earth, "giving pieces of my energy, love, healing . . ." He broke off again, saying in a dazed voice how he was just blown away to be getting through like this.

The knowledge of the realm of death makes it possible for the shaman to move freely back and forth and mediate these journeys for other people.

—STANISLAV GROF,
Czech psychiatrist

Chris was only forty-one years old at the time of his passing, and said that even though he'd been back in spirit for several years of earth time, he was still coming to terms with his passing. When he left his body he was very unhappy, thinking it was not his time, but has since come to accept the fact that it was. He still found it very difficult to be parted from his young daughter, Jamie, whom he doted on, describing this as like "having my heart torn out . . . just gut wrenching."

When I asked if he gets to see her often, his reply was typical of Chris, straight to the point. "Oh, shit yeah!" He visits her several times every day, saying he doesn't know how long it will take him to adjust to this separation. He referred to "a contract that was made, before I became Chris," and he had accepted that his passing with all its complications was part of that contract. However, he also said there was a big difference in knowing that, and what was going on emotionally for him.

Chris had also been a great inspiration for Kelly and his wife, Kristin, who spent six months in Brazil with John of God before setting up the Australian Casa in northern New South Wales as an official branch of John of God's Brazil casa. Chris helped Kelly and Kristin in their spiritual preparation to run this important healing center, and his abilities as a shaman were a powerful influence, as Chris spent many hours taking Kelly to new heights of awareness as his spiritual mentor. A magnificent 300-kilogram rose quartz crystal was imported from John of God's center in Brazil as the foundation stone of the Australian Casa. When the crystal arrived from Brazil, Chris and Kelly meditated sitting next to it, and the connection they experienced left them both in a very emotional state.

Chris said he has now been able to place part of his energy inside this crystal, which plays a significant role in the healing meditations conducted in the casa. The meditations are known as "current sessions" because of the energy generated by each participant, linking the group in spiritual healing. He explained that while every crystal has its own unique energy source, the extra energy that can be placed in this particular one enhances its abilities. Indigenous peoples know how to put this kind of energy into rocks and crystals of various sizes for their healing and ceremonial purposes. Chris cited Uluru in central Australia, such a spiritual and sacred place, as an example of this principle on a grand scale.

I asked Chris if he would mind talking about the journey he has made since he left his body. "Oh, no, that's why I'm here," he said with another chuckle.

He described his mind-set when he passed as being one of total shock. He realized he was parting with his body prematurely, and at the same time he was leaving behind his beloved daughter, Jamie, as well. He was distraught and felt he wasn't ready to leave at that time. "I hadn't realized how much of my heart I had sunk into Jamie, and when it was all taken away like that, it was a real shock." But now Chris has reluctantly accepted that it was something Jamie, too, had agreed to in her life contract. Still, it does not make their separation any easier.

Among his many activities Chris had been a spiritual teacher and practitioner in his earthly life. When he left his body he became aware that what he thought he knew spiritually was virtually nothing in the greater scheme of things. He described it as like becoming a baby again. The grief that he felt on passing was so strong that he needed time to work with it. He was met in spirit by Margaret Dent, a famous medium who had taken Chris under her wing and trained him many years earlier.

Margaret took Chris to connect with a group of old friends and family members in spirit, which he described as "like going to the pub for a school reunion." He walked through a doorway and saw many familiar faces, people he had not seen in a long time. They appeared to Chris exactly the way he had known them on earth, "same face, same person . . . just familiar-looking people and all looking happy and joyful . . . just a wonderful reunion with old friends."

The initial reaction for Chris was that it was so awesome, he actually forgot where he was for a while. "I totally forgot that I had passed over; it was just like being at a party." He described it as a feeling of coming home again, a sense of euphoria whose warmth and love were incredible. He caught up with many old friends, and some of those souls stayed with him in a spirit of mutual support as he settled into his new environment.

After that welcome-home celebration, Chris moved into a stage of learning. The healing he went through also included spending time with family and friends in spirit, which he described as being of great benefit.

"There is so much to learn here," he said. An important part of his learning was to find out why he had to die in the manner and circumstances he experienced. After several earth years in the afterlife, and despite working intensely with his soul group, he was still struggling to find all the answers. "I can't fully answer that question yet," he said a little sadly. Chris also revealed that he still found it difficult to cut his ties with the earth, although he had fully crossed over, and said that a lot of his energy continued "hanging around." He said he'd been given permission to do this until he was ready to move on more fully.

However, Chris did engage in many activities in the afterlife, including looking back at the stage of soul development he had achieved before starting his last incarnation. He chose not to elaborate on that very personal aspect of his development process. Part of his new life in spirit included communicating with various people on earth and passing on information about the afterlife. It was not surprising that

Chris was part of the group that worked with and provided energy and support to John Dingwall as its primary spokespirit.

Chris warned that there was much information to be communicated and said, "It's going to come thick and fast, not only from me, but others here." But just as we settled in for a long chat with Chris, we lost contact, which was extremely disappointing.

30

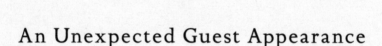

An Unexpected Guest Appearance

As this was his first communication since he crossed over, Chris Kelly could not sustain the energy level for long and he faded very quickly. We actually lost contact with him in midsentence, just as he was starting to talk about reconnecting with his soul family. This was very disappointing, as the energy levels had been very strong until then and Chris was on a roll. After Chris left, Kelly's wife, Kristin, and I sat for a few minutes wondering what was going to happen next, as this was breaking new ground in our afterlife contact via Kelly's trance medium sessions.

But it wasn't long before another spirit energy struggled through with seemingly a lot of difficulty. The entity sounded very weak and spoke in a soft whisper, describing itself as "a highly advanced spirit" who was there purely to play a part in spiritual communication. We knew that anyone coming through would have to be genuinely associated with John's group, as they were controlling the energy in spirit.

The spirit, who did not identify himself any further, sounded very pleased to be able to have the experience of being back in a human body, confirming he had enjoyed many lives on earth. The spirit had not been in human form for a very long time, saying, "My place is here."

After a short interval the spirit announced in a whisper even quieter than before, "I will depart," and with that the energy faded and was instantly gone. We later felt that this spirit just wanted to show us the depth of support we were receiving from the afterlife.

A few minutes later the spirit of John came through to wrap up the session, saying that he had been part of the support group holding the energy to allow these two contacts to happen. He told us that Chris had been trying to come through for quite some time, as was evident by the excitement he shared with us.

The communication that night had occurred on an eclipse, which John admitted certainly helped support the energy for bringing through the two spirits, but, he added, the timing was perfect overall to bring some others in his group through for the first time. After the session ended, Kristin and I were tempted to tell Kelly about his good friend Chris. However, we decided in the interests of any future contact to keep it to ourselves. Kelly also wished to read about these contacts when the book was published.

31

Illness and Life Contracts

Because of Kelly and Kristin's busy lifestyle with three children and a property to manage, it was not easy to schedule regular trance sessions. Sometimes many weeks would go by before we were able to get together to contact John Dingwall and the team again. This next session was one of those occasions, and we had all been looking forward to it for some weeks.

Greeting John's spirit when it first comes through in each sitting is like catching up with an old friend, as we have established a wonderful rapport during our many sessions. And just as one would greet an old friend, without thinking I asked him how he was, to which he replied, "Very well, very well."

A bizarre thought then struck me: Do spirits have health problems in the afterlife?

To my surprise, John confirmed that spirits do indeed get sick in the afterlife. And here I was, thinking all was perfect over there.

Spiritual sickness is not related to the physical terminology as we understand it on earth; no flu symptoms, upset stomachs, bloody noses, broken legs, or anything like that. Spirits experience sickness in an entirely different way. It will often manifest as a feeling of unease by which they immediately know that something is not right. John was speaking from his own experience, and confirmed this uneasy feeling is often related to what is happening to family and friends back on earth.

This particularly applies to those people who have recently returned to the afterlife. More advanced spirits have learned to cope with these feelings and not be so affected. John said that the best way to understand this condition is through the connection some spirits still feel to their human body, creating emotional reactions that take time to work through. My guide M describes it as an "energy disturbance."

Feelings and emotions related to our past incarnation do not just get cut off when we leave the body. Often a lot of anxieties cross over with us. Worries that spirits have about loved ones they have left behind can continue for a long time and are often related to the life contract that a spirit made before initially setting off on that life path. Spirits may have a sense of obligation, especially when those on earth are going through troubling times in their life.

So, how binding are the life contracts that we accept in spirit as part of a new incarnation, and are they still in place when we return to the afterlife?

According to John, life contracts can be very fluid; not all is predestined. If someone's circumstances change radically, new instructions are issued from Spirit, or perhaps another person takes over a particular responsibility, changing the dynamics of a situation. A release can also come into play, for example, when people on earth are able to become more independent and stand on their own two feet, having learned the life lesson they had accepted in their own contract.

Life contracts are made as a pre-life agreement with the Elders in spirit, and, if broken, are likely to have widespread effects. New karma could be created that will need to be dealt with at some point. It can mean soul lessons go unlearned, which often results in at least one more lifetime required to learn the lessons. The life that I experienced as the materialistic desert trader Arloon is a good example of this.

All we are doing is hurting ourselves when we knowingly break those contracts, because we are pushing ourselves into a corner, according to John. This means we do not move forward in our soul development, which is the main purpose of each life.

The question of associated karma occurred to me at this point. I had been wondering what would happen if two people had agreed to share a life to resolve a mutual karmic issue from a past life, and only one of them was able to complete that karma, through forgiveness, for example. Would the unresolved karmic issue with the second person have any impact on the first? Could it result in both having to come back for yet another lifetime to sort things out?

John confirmed that the first person in this case would move on, but the second one could have different options to resolve this resultant karma. There can be several different pathways to either teach or learn those lessons, and in these instances there is flexibility in the life contract. The tapestry of life that we discussed earlier is simply moved around so that another solution is available.

This tapestry, of which all our lives form a part, is so complicated that John admitted he is often bamboozled in trying to understand the ramifications of particular actions. The different paths, and the way things are connected at so many levels in everyone's lives, are quite astonishing. However, he said that in general other people's unresolved karma does not have to impact us, unless we condone it and so create new karma for ourselves.

32

Coincidence or Synchronicity?

We often get caught up in our lives by what are described as coincidences, strange events that attract certain elements or people to us. I have long since stopped using the word *coincidence*, preferring instead *synchronicity* or even *serendipity*. It is so easy to dismiss certain key events as merely being coincidental and not look for the significance of such occurrences.

So when John started to talk about the coincidences that occur in people's lives on earth, I questioned the term, asking whether *synchronicity* or *serendipity* was more appropriate. But John, ever the stickler for correct terminology, insisted that there are indeed coincidences. "It must be, because not everything is or can be planned, because we have free will and there will always be human error along the way, so even a small coincidence can dramatically change someone's path or their lesson." John went on to say that once again the three-dimensional jigsaw or tapestry of life comes into play in these circumstances, and those busy spirits behind the scenes have to reconfigure the path ahead, in what he described as a very complex system.

Having our spirit guides and helpers work with us during our lifetime is akin to having the backstage people such as producers, directors, and production crews on a film set who do a lot of the work but are rarely, if ever, seen by the audience. Sometimes there can be hundreds of spirits working together, albeit briefly, to achieve a particular goal. It is the ultimate example of teamwork.

A recent Hollywood movie, *The Adjustment Bureau*, embraced this theme, with men in suits, wearing hats and consulting clipboards, dashing around all over the place, making sure that people's predestined actions and circumstances went according to what had been ordained by the powers that be. If free will was unexpectedly exercised and things changed even minutely, adjustments were made accordingly by these hardworking entities. I was not surprised when my guide M said that the events in the film sometimes reflect the way our lives are influenced by Spirit.

The question of reincarnation emerged at this point, which, as previously discussed, often involves many lifetimes with the same group of people with whom we share experiences and soul growth opportunities. Reincarnation becomes part of a team effort for a defined purpose, frequently in times of need or desperation, according to John.

This spiritual jigsaw puzzle requires a great deal of pre-planning in the afterlife before these souls arrive back on earth, usually born in different years or generations, especially in the case of parents and children. If all these souls are sent back to reincarnate together, it means certain spirits in the afterlife, probably the Elders, have planned the future direction of the group as a whole. Sometimes the members of the group concerned are not given advance warning of the events that they will have to face. This, too, is part of the lessons they must learn in the upcoming lifetime.

John told us that most people in the afterlife are not as inquisitive as he, so questions of this nature are rarely asked. A screenwriter and journalist in his last incarnation, John described his life there as being like "a kid in a candy store," because he has access to vast amounts of knowledge. If one of his immediate contacts cannot supply answers, he is soon able to find someone who can, so he keeps asking questions.

He said it is just the same there as it is on earth, where some people are inquisitive and some are not, and this does not necessarily change once we return to the afterlife. When asked whether this was the reason why he is now the spokesman for the group we communicate with for this research, John replied enigmatically, "Who is to say that I did not agree to this before I went into the body as John?"

I think a lot more decisions are made on serendipity than
people think. Things come across their radar screens and
they jump at them.

—JAY W. LORSCH,
Louis Kirstein Professor of Human Relations
at the Harvard Business School

33

Predicting Your Future

Some of my erstwhile friends and colleagues in the media find it hard to accept that a former talk-show host, sports anchor, and newsreader can also be a clairvoyant and medium. Everybody has intuition. I just chose to develop mine to a higher state and work with it, but it doesn't make me a new-age flake or some psychic dropout. I enjoy helping people with my new abilities and also believe it has encouraged me to become a better person.

I was still working as a news presenter when a current-affairs magazine wrote a feature story about my astrology work. I knew my colleagues in the newsroom would see the article, and prepared myself for some ribbing on my next shift. To my surprise, not only did they accept my "other life" without question, several of them came to me for a consultation. One journalist mentioned in passing that he wrote an astrology column for a TV magazine for several years, as he was very interested in the practice.

Over the years I have done astrology and clairvoyant readings for a wide range of people, from truck drivers to psychologists. The thing they all have in common is the search for answers to problems in their lives, including questions about their future.

We all possess psychic abilities, but most people either do not believe they are intuitive or are simply not interested in developing these abilities. But how many people readily accept they have hunches or gut reactions?

People from all walks of life have uncovered their intuitive abilities in a multitude of ways, such as through special courses or simply by meditating deeply and allowing Spirit to help. Many leading clairvoyants and mediums discovered their latent ability only later in life, after working in other fields of endeavor. In some cases life circumstances give us the opportunity to develop our intuition. I had been working as a broadcaster for twenty-eight years before I opened the door to my psychic abilities, following the prediction of Diana Shaw, a brilliant clairvoyant who was cohosting a radio show with me. At first I thought she must be crazy, as I was running a media-relations company along with my radio and TV work at the time. But as it turned out, Spirit had other ideas, and I was the crazy one for doubting her!

Even science is climbing on the bandwagon of tuning in to the future. David Robson, writing in *New Scientist* magazine in October

2012, has noted, "Memory researchers have realized that the human memory did not evolve so that we could remember, but so that our minds could imagine what might be."

When we accept the roles that free will and destiny play in our lives, the question still remains: is it possible to predict the future with any degree of accuracy?

When I do a reading for people, I make sure they understand that predictions reflect the path they are currently traveling. It is like driving along a freeway to a chosen destination; if they choose to exit that road, they may head in another direction and create very different results. However, while destiny is always part of the picture, it is ultimately up to the person concerned to exercise free will.

We have previously discussed the buildup of events on a world basis that have gone out of control and led to major upheavals such as wars, economic crashes, and the like. Perhaps catastrophes like these are not difficult to predict. In fact, scientist Dr. Neil Hair, a regular guest on *Radio Out There*, accurately predicted the Global Financial Crisis of 2008 well in advance, using a combination of astrology and numerology.

John admitted that he is intrigued by the whole question of looking into the future, and described it as "the ultimate question" for many people on earth. This is why people consult clairvoyants, so that they can peer into their future and find answers for questions that are disturbing them. He also brought up again the subject of groups of souls reincarnating for a special purpose, and indicated that this can sometimes end up involving hundreds of thousands of people. He is fascinated by the knowledge that these events have been carefully planned by people in the afterlife who know in advance how this web of intrigue is potentially going to unfold.

When you add the influence of reincarnation to family trees, perhaps over many generations, it obviously requires very careful and detailed future planning. Particularly if certain members of the future family were on earth enjoying lifetimes with different groups when these plans were being formulated. (It feels to me more complicated than organizing the D-Day landings in France in 1944, enough to make my mind boggle.) In situations like that it would take an amazing intuitive ability for a psychic to work out the full picture and give appropriate guidance.

However, John believes this ingrained feeling of needing to know the future, perhaps left over from their planning days in the afterlife, is the reason people visit psychics and mediums.

John then came out with a statement that I have since thought a lot about. People in spirit express great fear about some psychics and mediums, he said. The problem is there are too many bad, untrained psychics and mediums who prey on people's emotions and needs, and consequently do a lot of damage. Their words are so powerful because they are dealing with people who are very vulnerable or at a crossroads in their life. Even if people consult a medium who they feel is a bit dubious, they still want to believe that the advice is coming from the afterlife.

"When you think about all the good work spirits are doing here, it can take a bad medium only a few minutes to undo it," he said. This is an area that seriously worries those in the afterlife, as they have no control over it. Lifetimes of good work can be undone in the blink of an eye. Apparently, the ripples that can be created by a bad reading can be disastrous for many people.

This problem came up again several months later when Anne and I did the weeklong residential course on mediumship at the world-famous Arthur Findlay College in the UK. The tutors there all expressed concern at the poor quality of many mediums practicing today and were determined to raise standards through the courses at the college. It's very easy for a so-called medium to say your grandmother, a white-haired old lady with glasses, says hello. Proof of identity is needed as well as messages that contain relevant information and support from the afterlife, and this takes a properly trained medium.

John did emphasize that there are many talented practitioners who are doing very good work, but they are being undermined by the charlatans, along with a lot of self-professed mediums who have "absolutely no connection with the afterlife." The main problem is that anyone can claim to be a psychic or a medium, with absolutely no ability to help others or connect with spirit. And some people are more concerned with making money than being of service. "Not everyone who hangs up their shingle is a good or even a genuine medium. Really good mediums are uncommon." It is important that people choose carefully and use their intuition before consulting anyone.

However, John insisted that even good mediums are not always able to interpret the messages being received from spirits as 100 percent accurate. This is especially the case with messages purportedly coming from animals; mediums often "muddle information being received from pets," which can be very misleading.

When I asked John about the information that I had recently received from Val Hood, a medium who connected with my late partner, Judy, he referred this to his advanced spiritual guide in the support group. The "control guide," as John referred to this spirit, confirmed that this was indeed a perfect connection. It was no coincidence that Val and I had been brought together. As Judy is also part of the team, I presume they also checked with her. The control guide added that there would be two other mediums that would be "thrown in my path" as part of the research for this book. I had previously spoken with my guide M, who gave me exactly the same message.

The sciences of astrology and numerology are recognized in spirit as positive sources of information, provided the practitioner has completed formal training in that body of knowledge and hasn't "just read a book about it and decided to set up shop." They are accepted in the afterlife as ancient sciences with time-honored accumulated knowledge, which, when coming from the right source, can be very beneficial for people.

The control guide further commented that fortunately there are many excellent psychics and mediums who are definitely helping those people who have nobody else to turn to and trust. The really good practitioners find that those in genuine need are guided to them for assistance. They quietly do their work in the community without asking for recognition. "The genuine ones that have real connection to spirit only have to walk into a room and focus their energy to make positive changes."

It seems the phrase *caveat emptor*, or "let the buyer beware," applies when you consult any source of intuitive guidance or counseling, as it does for most areas of life.

> *One day at a time—this is enough. Do not look back and*
> *grieve over the past, for it is gone: and do not be troubled*
> *about the future, for it has not yet come. Live in the present,*
> *and make it so beautiful that it will be worth remembering.*
>
> —IDA SCOTT TAYLOR, 1820–1915,
> author

34

Orbs and Spirit Images

The true mystery of the world is the visible, not the invisible.

—OSCAR WILDE, 1854–1900

In recent years, pictures of orbs of light floating around in the air have set tongues wagging, especially on the Internet. Digital photography has revealed these strange light forms in many different settings and countries, often seen hovering in the air in clusters around people.

There are popular theories that these orbs of light are in fact spirits returning to earth so that they can be around friends and family. I asked John if this was true.

"Absolutely not," he replied. "Despite what a lot of psychics say, orbs are not spirits."

I must confess that this surprised me; like many people, I had conveniently accepted the orbs-are-spirits theory.

John explained the sighting of orbs as the result of advanced camera technology and nothing more. He made an interesting point: "Sometimes when we get too advanced, we can see too much."

So then, if they are not spirits, what are these orbs?

According to John, orbs are simply matter, or to put it another way, pure energy. "It *is* spiritual energy, but they are not spiritual beings."

For those people who say they can see faces in orbs, John explained: "You can see a face wherever you want to see one—in orbs, clouds, smoke—and there is always the man in the moon."

John had told us earlier that spirits often see one another as orbs of light in the afterlife, but he still presents himself in the image of his most recent life, and he perceives others as he wants to see them. When spirits return to the afterlife, they naturally project themselves as an image of their most recent incarnation. As this is controlled by the power of thought, older people, or those affected by severe illness, usually prefer a younger image of themselves than how they appeared when they died. Young people can either show the image they had when they passed over, or choose to project themselves as growing older as earth time progresses. John added that the spirit of children who returned to the afterlife can still have lived many lifetimes and will then project whatever image they choose. However, some children have just returned from their first incarnation and will, as such, evolve in the afterlife with the help of their guides and other spirits.

On the other hand, spirits who are more advanced, or who have been back in the afterlife for a while, may choose to present themselves very differently. On occasion, John said, he feels an energy around him, which is like being tapped on the shoulder. Quite often he might see just a white mist, which he found "a little bit freaky" at first, or on other occasions he sees nothing at all. Once their presence is acknowledged, these spirits will then communicate by thought. They have been in the afterlife long enough not to feel the need to project an image of themselves.

Sometimes we can connect with a spirit, particularly in the dream state, and will recognize the person even though when we think about it later they appear nothing like our memory of them. John's explanation for this is that the spirits concerned may well want you to get used to them in what is really their generic spirit form. The last image we cherish is, in fact, just one of their incarnations and not necessarily the look they normally choose to project in the world of spirit. Once again, recognition is through the power of thought communication with each spirit.

When we get used to communicating with a spirit without bringing to mind their previous physical image, "things begin to open up." When we can get away from the association of that one previous lifetime, we can escape the limitations of that particular relationship and explore new ground. It is more important to relate to that person purely as a spirit, rather than with the restrictions and memories of an earthly relationship.

This becomes an important factor if we encounter a spirit that we had a relationship with hundreds or even thousands of earth years ago. As we may have had no contact with it for countless lifetimes, it would be useless for that spirit to project an image of its last incarnation to us. John brought up his own situation as a case in point by saying that he did not have to communicate to us as the man we knew as John Dingwall. "I am now talking to you as a spirit, but you feel more comfortable speaking to me as John because you knew me in that life." He also still felt the need to converse as John, but that would change. He rather enigmatically mentioned that if this did occur, it would radically alter the nature of our channeling sessions, because "John" was just one of his many incarnations.

He added that in the afterlife he could be hailed by a spirit with whom he had shared a past life, many lifetimes ago, so having a generic spirit image would make sense. While this has happened to him on quite a few occasions, he said that embracing a generic spirit image is something that is best done gradually so that homecoming spirits can avoid great confusion.

John summed it up rather colorfully: "If you had an overload when you first return, you wouldn't be able to handle it and you might explode."

The vision of an exploding spirit produced great hilarity on both sides of the divide, and brought that particular session to an unscheduled but pleasant conclusion.

35

∞

Contacting Earth

When loved ones pass over, those of us left behind can have a feeling of devastating loss, believing we will have no further contact with them while we are still on earth. But, as John and the team have confirmed, spirits are able to return to visit us with the permission of their guides, to whisper in our ear, keep an eye on us, or just send loving energy. Communication in the afterlife is by thought, as spirits have no physical body or voice, so often we will suddenly think of loved ones in spirit or feel their energy around us.

In this day and age of advanced technology, spirits are contacting their loved ones in new, unusual ways. I was approached at a writers' festival by a woman who wanted to share a contact experience. She was dumbfounded to receive an e-mail from a loved one in spirit, and that a message could find its way to her in this manner. She told me the content of this very detailed and personal message, which included a quote that nobody apart from the two of them would know about, and so confirmed for her beyond a doubt that it was indeed from her loved one. I had heard of spirits using the telephone to get in touch, but this was the first example of their using the Internet.

When I put this to John, he confirmed that messages can be passed through the Internet, and the fact that we are able to share this information in this book could well be the reason it was delivered in this manner. It could open up new lines of communication that will affect thousands of people. Another way that spirits are communicating directly is through a process known as electronic voice production, or EVP. The most common method of contact is to set up a digital recorder in a quiet space and time, usually in the early hours, and simply let it record for a while. Before recording, meditation or quiet time, while asking for contact from the afterlife, is important.

Many years ago I interviewed Judith Chisholm in the UK for my program, *Radio Out There*. Judith had *accidentally* recorded a spirit voice while she was taping a séance, trying to contact her son in the afterlife. In between the voices of the people present, she heard her name being clearly whispered by a woman. Judith was the only woman in the group that night, and she knew she did not whisper her own name, so it had to be a voice from spirit.

When Judith researched this phenomenon, she found that EVP

was accidentally discovered by Friedrich Jürgenson in 1959.[1] One day Jürgenson, a Swedish artist and film producer, was filming alone in nature, but when he listened back to the audio there was a man's voice overlaying the bird calls he was recording. Annoyed by this at first, he continued his recordings, but the problem persisted. His subsequent tapes contained other voices, some calling him by name and others referring to family members in spirit. He was finally convinced the voices were from the afterlife when his mother came through, saying "Friedel," her pet name for him. He later published a book, *Voices from the Universe.*

Judith continued with her experiments and was eventually able to communicate with her son Paul in the spirit world, as well as speaking with other family members. EVP has been adopted by many people, and with the digital technology we now enjoy, the quality of voice recordings is bound to improve.

I decided to test this theory, and late one night I turned on the digital recorder in an empty bedroom to see what I could pick up. The best time is around two or three in the morning, as the energies are at their quietest then. There were no voices when I replayed the disk, but when I boosted the volume, the distinct sounds of a heavenly choir could be heard in the distance. It was a beautiful sound that could only have come from the spirit world, as there were no choirs around my house that night.

I received an emotional but heartwarming e-mail from Dale in Canada after she read *Afterlife.* Dale's son Greg passed over early in

2012 from a rare disorder of the brain. Greg was admitted to a hospital after a series of strokes and passed over eight days later. He was unable to speak while in the hospital, and could move only his right hand. However, his mother then saw something that, despite her son's condition, amazed and delighted her. Greg's eyes had turned a dazzling blue, and when Dale looked at him she could see "the absolute purity of his spirit." Greg then surrounded his family with a strong, loving energy that impacted everyone present. The minister who was in the room was so affected by this energy he spoke about it at Greg's funeral service.

Shortly after Greg went into the hospital, Dale bought a new smartphone, which several months later Greg utilized from the afterlife to let his family know that he was alive in spirit and well. All kinds of weird things started happening to the phone: the screen became stuck, and nothing could be done with it for a while. Then Dale discovered that a copy of a holiday video clip had suddenly appeared on her new phone that Greg had shot on another camera two years before his death. These mysterious contacts continued, culminating with the camera on the phone suddenly clicking when Dale and her youngest son, Darren, were looking at the screen and a picture of Greg miraculously appeared from nowhere. Dale sent me a photo of the phone with Greg's picture, which shows the time and date. My guide M confirmed that Greg is an advanced spirit and is able to communicate this way.

The story then took a new twist. While I was composing an e-mail to Dale, her son Greg came through to me from spirit together with an energy that I identified as a grandmother. They showed me a picture of a patchwork quilt and asked me to tell Dale. Greg then sent me an image of him holding his hands to his throat and smiling, saying that now he has no further breathing problems.

I knew that Dale and her family were still deeply grieving, so I debated whether to send them this information. We had been in communication only by e-mail, and I didn't want to upset them further if this information didn't ring true for them. My guide M came to the rescue and encouraged me to tell Dale of my contact. So I did.

The next day I received this reply from Dale:

> You cannot imagine how deeply your message means to my son Darren, my husband, Duane, and myself. Everything you posted about Greg was so accurate that it almost overwhelmed me all day yesterday.
>
> The grandmother energy and the patchwork quilt. Definitely, this would be my mother who passed years ago. This in itself was amazing but I wondered about Mom being there for Greg and she was—is. The patchwork quilt was made by my mother for Greg's crib. One of the last times Greg visited me before the illness set in, we had this friendly banter about the articles Mom had made him and I was desperately trying to get him to choose between a sweater Mom had knitted for him or the quilt. One article was to go to Darren because Mom passed away before she

could do anything for Darren, the youngest. At the end of the banter, Greg decided he'd keep the quilt.

Your description of Greg holding his throat and wanting me to know his breathing is healed touched my soul because he was indeed having breathing problems. Having to witness what Greg was going through was the toughest ordeal my son Darren and I could possibly experience. That Greg is smiling makes us so happy. That he has found peace is a gift we'll not soon forget.

We love and miss him. You have given us such an inspirational insight of where Greg is and who is with him.

Dale's response touched my soul and shows that the link between earth and the Heaven World not only has many channels of communication but is always open to us. Spirit works in wondrous ways.

Other people have reported receiving telephone calls from a loved one recently deceased, and I have also heard of messages from spirit that have been left on answering machines, long after that person had passed. As yet, I have heard no stories of Facebook messages or Tweeting from spirit, which could be a blessing.

The question remains, how do spirits manage to communicate by voice in this manner when they have no voice box? My guide M informed me spirits are able to project their thoughts into these physical devices the same way that they utilize the physical body of a trance medium. This would also explain why the voices recorded with EVP are sometimes very fuzzy when they are replayed.

I guess that when it comes to getting messages across, a spirit has to do what a spirit has to do.

The artist alone sees spirits. But after he has told of their appearing to him, everybody sees them.

—JOHANN WOLFGANG VON GOETHE, 1749–1832

36

<hr/>

To Sleep, Perchance to Dream

Dreams are illustrations . . . from the book your soul is writing about you.

—MARSHA NORMAN,
author and screenwriter

It seems that the most popular form of communication from our loved ones in spirit is through our dreams. Most people at some stage dream about a loved one who has passed over, even if they don't remember much about the details when they wake up the next morning. Sometimes they just *know* they've dreamed about the person, but recall nothing else; they just have a fuzzy memory. That is why many people find it difficult to accept that it was a spirit contact.

While the body needs to rest, the spirit—being pure energy—does not, and so it leaves the physical form to go roaming while we are asleep. Our spirit can connect with our guide for some assistance, head off to explore some other reality, or, when conditions are right, make contact with those in the afterlife, including members of its own soul group. So the dream state is a perfect opportunity for departed spirits to connect and let family and close friends on earth know they still exist and have not disappeared into some black hole. Once contact has been established, they can also pass on other information through dreams. Of course, it is up to the recipient whether or not to take advantage of this information.

Most people I have spoken to are delighted with any evidence of survival and accept that dreams are a form of contact with loved ones. My parents came back to visit me only once, just to let me know they were okay, contacting me several months after each one passed over. My father came most unexpectedly in a dream when I was in Tahiti, hosting a group of travel journalists, and I was certainly not thinking about him at the time, having been out celebrating that night. My mother appeared and sat on the end of my bed one night and quietly connected with me before slipping away back to her spiritual home. I have never seen or heard from my mother again, so I guess she figured that was enough for all our purposes. However, my father recently made contact again through the medium Ezio De Angelis, which I discuss in chapter 40.

Survival evidence from spirit can be very comforting, but I believe our loved ones usually also have a message for us, especially when they come through a medium. Patrick, a guest on *Radio Out There* and who is part of a dream network in the United States, told me of a dream he had had when he was only sixteen years old, shortly after the death of his father. In the dream Patrick saw his father in a field, holding red flowers, looking happier than he could ever remember him being during his life. Patrick commented that his father also looked a lot younger in the dream than when he died. This is usually the case, as most people in the afterlife choose to show themselves at their best, usually the way they looked at around thirty years of age. His father gave Patrick a simple message for each member of the family and told him to read a book by a French author with a surname starting with S, which he could not remember the next day. Years later, while reading a book by Jean-Paul Sartre while he was in Paris, Patrick had a flashback to his dream and realized this was the book referred to by his father.

Not only do we have dream contact with our family and friends, but our guides often use dreams to send us lessons and information we need to know. I woke one morning with the name of an old friend resounding in my mind. This was someone I had not seen, or even thought about, in many years, but I knew I had to get in touch. I rang him later that day and he was most surprised as he, too, had been thinking about me a couple of days prior. He had some information for me that was very relevant to a project that I was involved in at the time. I believe these thoughts and suggestions are often given to us by our guides, as well as our loved ones in the afterlife, as a form of telepathy, and it is up to us to follow through. If we are so preoccupied with everyday concerns that we ignore an important message, we may lose out on opportunities or suffer a negative impact. When we ignore messages or guidance, it can often be repeated in a much stronger way, almost forcing us to take notice.

Patrick also told me of another dream that he had, one that demonstrated to him some of the difficulties of communication from the spirit world. He described the spirit of a man he knew who had recently passed over who was valiantly trying to communicate with his family on earth. His lack of success made him very frustrated, as his family were not picking up his thoughts. Patrick's dream revealed this spirit was subsequently coached by his guide and told he was using too much force, and to try more subtle means to communicate. Patrick took this as a sign to help facilitate his own dream contacts a little better.

Sometimes dream contact can happen many years after someone has crossed over. I had a vivid dream about David Paterson, an old friend from my commercial radio days, while I was putting the finishing touches to *No Goodbyes*. David, or "Pato," as he was known to his friends, had passed suddenly in the early 1990s while only in his fifties. In addition to hosting radio programs, David and his wife, Helen, had purchased a property in the Hunter Valley winegrowing area in Australia and started their own vineyard. Pato was always a great wine buff, and he and I even ran our own food and wine club at one stage, hosting some of the great winegrowers of the time. David was able to produce some excellent-quality wines from his appropriately named vineyard, Chateau Pato. He and Helen had two sons, Nicholas and Michael, and Nicholas inherited his father's love of wine-growing.

Over the years I have tried to contact Pato in the afterlife on many occasions, with absolutely no success. Then suddenly he came to me in a dream, full of life, with a strong message. "Please contact Helen with a message for Nicholas. I want him to know how proud I am of him." I awoke from this dream with his words ringing in my ears, and when I switched on the bedside light I saw it was just after three a.m. I could feel Pato's presence very strongly around me and was able to communicate with his spirit. I asked him why he had taken so long to contact me, despite my many efforts. His reply was typical of Pato: "I had a lot of exploring to do first." I later realized that this was the exploration of the self as opposed to some afterlife jungle expeditions. His energy faded, and after thinking about his visit for a while I finally managed to get back to sleep.

When I awoke at around seven a.m. I could still feel David's presence, and once again his words formed in my thoughts. "Come on, Von Eaton [his nickname for me], ring Helen. I want Nicholas to know how proud I am of him."

Not wanting to ring Helen so early in the morning, I waited for half an hour before giving in to his impatience. I could almost hear Pato saying, "Come on, just give her a ring, don't worry about the time." It was all right for him in a timeless world!

I hadn't been in contact with Helen for at least eight or nine years, so she was a little surprised by my early-morning phone call, to say the least. However, when I told her that I had a message from David, she became very excited. She later told me that she often felt David's presence around her and hadn't stopped talking to him since he passed over. But she had not had a direct communication in all that time, except in her dreams.

When I told her that David wanted to especially recognize Nicholas and say how proud he was of him, Helen went very quiet. I asked her if she knew why Pato wanted to get a message to his son. Was Nicholas doing something special?

Choking back the tears, Helen told me that Nicholas had recently been given the Hunter Valley Winemaker of the Year Award for 2012, the highest honor of the region. Nicholas was coming to see her that morning and she would now be able to pass on his father's congratulations. Nicholas and David had always had a very strong bond, one that has obviously stood the test of separation.

We both then realized how Pato had been keeping abreast of his family all the time he had been in the afterlife. Helen then added that in a couple of weeks' time it would be the twentieth anniversary of David's passing. He obviously wanted to share so much with his family, and I felt honored that I was able to be the bearer of such good news.

Sometimes we try too hard to contact our loved ones in spirit and feel disappointed when nothing happens.

My guide M says that if you want to contact someone in the afterlife, relax, meditate, hold a picture of the person in your mind, ask for help from your guide, trust, and let it happen. You may get a picture in your mind, a voice, relevant thoughts, or sometimes just a knowing. It may not be easy at first, so be patient and be prepared to give it several attempts. When you are stressed and the mind is racing, it is almost impossible to connect across the divide.

And always remember the importance of your dreams.

Part Four

Judy

37

A Very Special Valentine's Day

Several months passed before I was able to get together with Val Hood, the UK medium who had connected so clearly with Judy in the afterlife. As I wrote in chapter 10, "Judy's Surprise," both Val and I were speakers at a special afterlife presentation the previous year, when Judy took the opportunity to connect strongly while Val was demonstrating her medium skills. In the meantime, heeding Judy's words of encouragement, I had started writing this book, and more information soon flowed from many different directions.

There were so many questions I wanted to put to Judy, who by now had been back in the afterlife for nearly fifteen earth years. I had received a few messages via dreams and meditation, but until Val connected with her so clearly in her demonstration, there had been no direct contact for several years. The connection that Val made with Judy was full of wonderful messages, but all too brief for me after such a long time. However, it whetted my appetite for a longer connection, so eventually I was able to arrange a private session with Val.

At this stage Val was staying with friends in a city about 1,800 kilometers from where I live, so it meant a plane trip, and also finding the best place to hold a meeting. The effort involved only increased my expectations, and by the time I caught up with Val, my sense of anticipation was high.

We decided the best place to have our session was at the hotel where Anne and I were staying, so I set up my recording gear, as I didn't want to risk losing a word from Judy after all this time. Contact with the afterlife can often play havoc with technical gear as I have found in the past, doing live talkback radio, so I set up two different recording devices for our session. Having traveled so far for this special occasion, I was not about to take any chances.

Just to prove a point, one recorder worked perfectly, but the audio software on my laptop computer played up at first, and then the recording became so distorted that it eventually had to be scrapped. Similar technical mishaps often happen with microphones when mediums are doing stage presentations, clearly showing the different levels of vibration between our two worlds. On earth our energy vibrates at a very dense level, much slower than vibrations in the world of spirit. When spirits come into our dimension they have to lower their vibration rate significantly to communicate. Some spirits come through with a very high energy level, which can affect electronic equipment.

Sometimes initial contact can take a little while to stabilize; however, Judy was there straightaway, and her spirit energy had actually been accompanying Val for a couple of hours beforehand. Judy was obviously very keen to make contact. Val told me later that she had been nervous about making the connection with Judy, knowing how important it was for me, until she heard a voice saying, "Will you stop worrying, it's going to be fine." Not surprising for me, as Judy had always been one to take charge.

Our meeting was held most appropriately on St. Valentine's Day, and Judy came through very emotionally at first, saying that it meant a lot to her to be able to connect on this special day. She warned me that despite our relationship on earth, I had to realize her essence in the world of spirit is not the person that I knew when we were together. Judy was apparently very excitedly showing Val picture after picture in her mind, and they were coming so quickly that Val threw up her hands and asked her to slow down. Val then closed her eyes and told me that she saw five people standing around me in the room. She recognized them as guides who were there to help her receive the messages from Judy. She was later told that they were also some of Judy's soul support group.

Suddenly there were several seconds of complete silence as Judy dramatically demonstrated what had happened immediately after she passed over. "There was a long period of silence because of the way I passed," she told us. Judy had died after a short illness at the age of only fifty-one from a rare heart-lung condition, in which she suffered terrible breathing difficulties. Judy told us that she needed a period of complete peace when she first crossed over because she felt "shattered into tiny fragments" and required healing to be put back together, to raise her spiritual level to a higher vibration.

Judy's whole life had been an emotional roller coaster, and she needed this recovery period to help her settle into the afterlife again. She revealed that this had been her last lifetime on earth and that in such cases, "They throw everything at you, and it is your biggest test." She told us that members of her soul support group have that in common, as they have all endured a very tough lifetime on earth, and are now ready to work to get this story of the afterlife out to as many people as possible.

Judy spoke about the moment she first left her body, describing her experience as a sense of floating, in which she was "being met and taken," but she didn't realize at the time where she was being moved. At this stage of the soul's entry back into the afterlife, they are taken to a healing center to recover from any illnesses or health conditions that have been imprinted on the spirit body after it detaches from the physical.

The next vision she showed Val was a long white room that appeared almost as if it had been made of ice. There were windows in the room, but they were like dark spaces, and Val could not see through them. Judy soon discovered that each dark space contained one of the key lessons she was supposed to have learned in her last life.

Judy was referring to the life-review process that every returning spirit faces. Every soul experiences this review in its own unique way. Each portal took Judy into a different period of her previous life, starting when she was only three years old. She then looked at her life at various stages, having been shown the events of each particular time and how she had dealt with key situations that had arisen. Judy was able to tell us that when she emerged from this review she found out she had passed with flying colors, even though she admitted that in some of her lessons she had not done too well. However, by the time she had reached the end of her life, even though she was still young by today's standards, she had accomplished everything that she was meant to achieve. Judy knew at her time of passing that she had done her best and was happy with the way she had conducted her life. She realized after crossing over that she was ready to move on, and didn't need her physical body anymore.

It was an important confirmation for me that when the soul decides it has no further need of the body to which it is attached, the spirit lets go and moves back into the afterlife. As the soul attaches itself to our body at the heart, this detachment is an emotional release.

Judy then confirmed that she and I, as soul mates, had met again in the last few years of her life, as was our destiny, so that she could complete her final incarnation.

At this point Val felt Judy touching her on the arm, which she interpreted as Judy's way of telling her that I had become her right arm in the last months of her life. Val had no way of knowing that I nursed Judy through her final weeks at home, with help from other members of her family. Judy wanted me to know that she appreciated my support in helping her cope with those last, painful days of her life.

Judy acknowledged that while those last few weeks on earth had seemed to me to go on forever, for her everything sped up and "it was over in a flash." She needed the peace of those last days and hours to reconcile her life.

After initially being sent home in a highly emotional state from the hospital when the doctors bluntly told her they could do nothing further for her, Judy's condition deteriorated rapidly. She went into respite care two months later for what I thought was to be only a few days, but she passed away quietly in the early hours of the morning, only a few hours after being admitted. Right to the end, I had believed that there would be some miracle and she would recover. It took me many, many months to accept that this was her time to go.

While recalling the details of her passing and her arrival in the afterlife, Judy indirectly confirmed something that I had always wondered about. Peter Ramster, the psychologist, good friend, and past-life expert, who was treating Judy in her last weeks, had dreamed about her final moment on earth the night before she passed. Peter had become close to Judy and believed that she was healing. In the dream he saw two beings come through the window beside her hospital bed and gently help her spirit leave her body before all three turned into white doves and flew away. Both Peter and I felt the doves were angelic symbols.

It was a beautiful image and a very prophetic dream—Peter did not even know that Judy was in the hospital, let alone the fact that her bed was the only one situated next to the window in the large ward.

Suddenly Val asked me if I "had a thing" for angels, and I confirmed this, as I often tune in to the angelic realm for help and guidance. Judy then confirmed that angels are real, which my guide M later said was her way of verifying Peter's dream.

Nowadays even presidents, vice presidents, and heads of
big agencies are opening their minds to accept psychic
phenomena, because they know they work.

—URI GELLER,
psychic

38

Information from the Akashic Records

As Val's contact with Judy became stronger with each passing minute, so too did the scope of the information being received. When our session first started, Judy asked me to write down any questions I wanted her to answer, in what turned out to be a very long and detailed communication.

However, after speaking about her passing, Judy needed no further prompting, as she had arrived with a program of information that she wanted to cover. She spoke about spirits accessing information about past incarnations stored in the Hall of Knowledge, often referred to as the Akashic Records. I had previously experienced this hall as a classically designed building, which I visited in my previous between-life journey as Brian. Judy described it as huge, vast, bigger than I could imagine. She then revealed that the Hall of Knowledge is not tucked away in some corner of the spirit world; it is actually inside each one of us. It is around us all the time, even when we are in our physical body.

This was the first time I had heard this concept and it opened up a whole new direction in my imagination. It had been easy to create an image of some kind of building in the afterlife, storing massive amounts of information, like some gargantuan warehouse. This was a whole different ball game. Judy's explanation of our inner space showed me how our limited thinking makes it so difficult for us to understand the power of spirit. We have conditioned our minds to see a solid structure to know that something like a hall of records could actually exist.

But when I thought about it later, the idea made a lot of sense, because we create so much in the afterlife using the power of thought. If we have a storehouse of information contained within us, it also explains how we are able to access our storehouse of wisdom and also recall our past lives.

We can also train ourselves to access the Akashic Records without relying on a specially trained medium, starting off by learning how to raise our energy vibrations to a higher level. My guide M confirmed that our guides can help us to do this when they decide that we are ready.

The Akashic Record is like an immense photographic film,
registering all the desires and earth experiences of our planet.

—ALICE A. BAILEY, 1880–1949,
author of *The Light of the Soul*

But once we are back in spirit, our visit to the Hall of Records becomes a different and more intense experience. Judy showed Val images of people floating up and down in a vast space, while others were clad in dark cloaks hiding their faces. Val also noted that these spirits had no feet. Judy was demonstrating how people move around in the afterlife, using nothing more than the power of thought.

Judy also spoke about spirits being around us all the time as we go about our lives on earth, but we can't see them because they are on a higher vibratory level. She also said that the world of spirit is located just above our own, and my guide M later described it colorfully as "sort of like icing on a cake."

Judy told us she has advanced to the stage where she is now able to be in hundreds of places at the same time. Part of her activities in the afterlife include working with spirit children in the healing center after they first cross over. She also works with new souls who have to choose some of the lessons they wish to learn, and because of her experience and the level she has attained in the spirit world, she is able to help them with their planning. She explained that new souls are being created all the time, which answers the question many people ask about the burgeoning world population and the number of souls needed to supply the demand.

The creation of new souls is a fascinating procedure, one that Judy was able to explain in graphic detail. She showed Val an image of a light being shattered into many fragments, with a solid part remaining intact at the core. This very dense core of energy embodies old souls, and those fragments exploding to the outside represent newer souls. We are all part of the same original spirit and the spirit fragments spread outward with the newest souls on the outer fringes.

Judy explained further, "When this shattering takes place, part of our soul heals and stays in spirit and another part moves on, so we go into different areas. The new souls are the less dense parts of that spirit energy." This means there is a part of every soul in each new one created, as we are all growing, all evolving, at all times.

At this stage, as my head was spinning with thoughts and images of all these fragments, M came to my rescue, saying that this explains the oneness of all life. The original energy that fragmented, creating the first souls, is what most people refer to as "God" (also the Creator, the Divine, the Source, Spirit). Each fragment then becomes its own spirit entity, before eventually fragmenting again, and so on. M also explained that new souls come from only the more advanced spirits; I found it comforting to know that spirits in the dark side are not given this capability. It also explains, for me, why so many gifted children are being born in recent years—their deep soul wisdom and advanced intelligence are sorely needed in the future to help us in these turbulent times.

Judy provided Val with the well-known image of an onion to further illustrate her point. The core of the onion is surrounded by many layers, which can peel off and have an application of their own. The core stays the same, growing new layers as they are needed. The core represents our true self, while the various layers develop their own paths. Each layer finds its own direction, which will include another incarnation and ultimately the creation of a new soul. These layers will eventually return to the core soul to "do it all again." Judy's soul essence—her core—with whom we were communicating was attached to her body—a layer—in her last life; otherwise, she said, I would not be able to recognize her. But it doesn't matter how much we fragment, our core essence is still always there in the world of spirit.

This fragmentation happens to every soul when it reaches a certain stage of development, but the number of times we are able to splinter depends on the density of the core spirit itself. As each soul learns and grows from its many incarnations, it is able to embrace the core spirit more closely each time it returns, until it has no further need to reincarnate. This core spirit is referred to by several names: the oversoul, the soul energy, and also the higher self. It is always with us during our physical life, but the majority of people do not realize this. We can learn how to tap into the wisdom and guidance of the core spirit through meditation and the power of intention.

Each soul group has to explore and undergo every possible earthly experience through its various members, and new souls are created for this purpose. As each soul ends its earthly life cycle, the last incarnation is usually the most complex of them all. Many challenges and difficult life conditions are usually part of this final experience for these "old souls." On the other hand, new souls may float through life with no apparent problems, where everything is seemingly handed to them on a plate, partly because they have no accumulated karma. However, as they create karmic lessons on their first trip to earth, each subsequent incarnation will become more complicated. So, I guess, the message for these new souls is, enjoy the easy life while you can!

M added that the core spirit becomes denser as souls become more advanced through their many incarnations.

Judy's description of fragmentation also means that the life I am consciously living right now is probably only one of several other aspects that my soul energy is simultaneously experiencing, not only on earth but also in other dimensions of reality. This explanation made it clearer to me how we are able to reincarnate with the same souls over many lifetimes, as our soul groups are actually part of the same core energy.

Judy also confirmed that she and I are aspects of the same soul, as are various other members of my earthly family. She refused to identify them, saying that if she told me it would spoil it for everyone. Recognition has to be at a soul level, not just in the head. The only person she would confirm as part of this core group is my partner, Anne, because, as Judy put it, "you knew that anyway."

For me this explanation finally defines a concept of soul mates to which I can relate.

39

The Heavenly World of Judy

When I spoke with Judy I was delighted to hear about her life in spirit, particularly as we had parted under such emotional circumstances. While we'd had brief conversations and some dream contact, this was the first opportunity I had to really communicate with her for many years. A few months after she crossed over she contacted me through the medium Ruth Phillips, after which I was told we had been given permission by the powers that be to stay in contact. My abilities as a medium started to develop, and when I look back on it now, I realize Spirit was setting the wheels in motion for me to write books on the afterlife.

As I prepared to speak with Judy through Val Hood, I already knew that our activities in the afterlife are many and varied, with opportunities for advancement to higher planes available for everyone. We are required to expand our self-knowledge, and also work with other souls in their development, both in the world of spirit and also on earth wherever appropriate.

Judy told me that she loves working with the spirits of children who have passed over and are going through the healing center before returning to their soul groups. She is also an important member of the soul group with John Dingwall as its spokespirit as they channel themselves through trance medium Kelly Dale, offering us their collective wisdom and experience.

I was disappointed that she had not come through directly in one of our group sessions, but M informs me that this will happen in the future. I do remember one occasion, several years before John started to communicate, when Kelly and I were working on developing his trance mediumship. Kelly had communicated with his guide, and then suddenly his whole demeanor changed and Judy unexpectedly came through. I must admit it was a bit strange to watch Kelly's face melt a little and hear a soft, almost feminine voice, full of emotion, spill from his lips. Judy had a few very personal messages for me, and I, too, was filled with emotion at her unanticipated presence. Perhaps the whole experience was a little strange for Judy as well, because she has never come through this way again.

Judy was always very house-proud in her last life, and a week or so before she passed, I discovered her on her hands and knees cleaning the bathroom, despite her intense breathing difficulties, because people were coming to visit. I was horrified, but obviously my puny efforts at domestic maintenance were rubbish in her estimation.

It came as no great surprise when I visited her in the dream state, a year or so after she passed over, that the first thing she wanted to show me was her house. Using the power of thought, she had created a classic rose-covered cottage with a lovely garden, set in a verdant valley, surrounded by rolling hills. I remember mischievously going outside this very neat little cottage, where I created snow with my thoughts, making a snowball. I then brought it inside and threw it at her, snow splattering all over the place. She pretended to be very annoyed at me and we both had a good laugh. At that point I sat bolt upright in bed, vividly recalling my "dream" as tears poured down my cheeks. That dream has stayed in my mind, and many years later it is still as clear as the night I experienced it.

So it was a lovely confirmation when Val Hood told me that Judy loved working in her garden and was surrounded by flowers of every variety, with colors that Val could see but not describe, as they were unlike any we knew on earth.

Judy was born under the astrological sign of Scorpio in her last life and typically enjoyed mysteries, secrets, and delving into the past. In the spirit world she has explored her past lives and told us that she had been a preacher in one incarnation. She mentioned that as I had been a priest in one of my lives, this demonstrates how the group soul sends out its emissaries to explore every facet of life.

Judy loved to travel, and in her spirit life she now indulges that interest, combining it with offering help and support to those people in great need in "ravaged countries." She told us that during her many lives on earth she never felt she was able to do enough for other people, and is making up for it with her afterlife activities.

Never one to hold back her thoughts, Judy went on to say that in her soul group situation they are also trying to help various communities in need, but that "politicians the world over have the same idiotic mentality." She said the big changes that are coming in the world are not going to be brought about by politicians, because people themselves will need to "get down and dirty, go back to grass roots," and politicians don't work that way. There will be a lot of confusion, but people will be guided from spirit on how to change their lives, and certain individuals are now being placed in key positions where they will be able to help and organize things when the changes come.

It was a joy to be able to hold such a long conversation with Judy in spirit, especially on Valentine's Day. Afterward, on a day that seemed sunnier than normal, Val, Anne, and I had lunch in a lovely restaurant overlooking the river. The spirit contact was longer than usual for Val, and she expressed her amazement at the intensity of information that Judy had sent through. She had never heard about the fragmentation of the soul in such graphic detail, and it opened a whole new line of thought for her. Val is one of the finest mediums I have worked with, and it was indeed a pleasure to hear her speak about the information she received in this way.

40

∞

Judy's Funeral and Beyond

Funeral pomp is more for the vanity of the living than for
the honor of the dead.

—FRANÇOIS DE LA ROCHEFOUCAULD, 1613–1680,
Fre n c h writer

Most spirits choose to stay around for their funeral after they leave
the body. Whether it is to complete their life and say goodbye to loved
ones or just to see who turns up on the day, it is a widespread practice.
My spirit guides tell me it is a lot easier for souls to fully cross over
after their funeral, as they have a sense of completion and are now
ready to embark on the next stage of their life.

Judy's funeral was one of the worst days of my life. Her family were too grief-stricken to speak and insisted that I do the oratory. The parish priest was away and the stand-in for the ceremony did not know Judy, and, even worse, stumbled over his words and had to keep referring to his notes to remember her name. This upset me further, but strangely enough it also gave me the strength to get through the ordeal. When I said that neither Judy nor I was religious, but held strong spiritual beliefs, the glare I received from the priest almost made me laugh. Ruth Phillips had given me a wonderful piece of prose for the oratory, which I was able to read without breaking down. Ruth saw Judy's spirit accompany the coffin as it was wheeled down to the altar by four ladies dressed in white. Judy then came to join me for the oratory, and linked her arm through mine, providing the extra strength I needed. What a blessing to have a wonderful medium and friend like Ruth at the funeral!

There were so many things I wanted to speak to Judy about, and the contact with her through Val Hood was delightful, but far too brief for me.

After being told in one of the sessions with John's group that I would be in contact with two or three mediums to get Judy's full story, I felt intuitively that Ezio De Angelis, one of Australia's best mediums, was the perfect choice. Ezio and I had worked together on radio and also in a couple of stage appearances, and I had seen firsthand his special abilities to contact spirits in the afterlife, and tap into several layers of information. Ezio and his wife, Michelle, had also asked me to launch their book, *Postcards from the Other Side,*[1] which contains some wonderful and moving stories from the afterlife.

Once again, the session involved traveling, this time returning to the city of my birth to see Ezio, and I had plenty of time to anticipate another chat with Judy. When I arrived at his rooms, we both admitted we were full of nervous anticipation. Ezio had officially launched *After-life* and knew about my relationship with Judy, but had never met her.

I shook my head in amazement when the first person to come through in our sitting identified himself as Ernie, my late father-in-law from my second marriage. Ernie told Ezio that he was acting as the "gatekeeper" on this occasion, and after sending his best wishes he ushered Judy through the veil that separates our two realities. His cheery words of support were a testimony to the fact that people in spirit do not hold grudges, as I had not communicated with him in any way since I split up with his daughter Carol in 1990.

Without any prompting on my part, Judy's first words to Ezio were that she had crossed over easily after the funeral and has been around me as a guardian angel ever since. Judy revealed that my anguish and soul-searching that followed her passing were actually a part of my preparation to be able to write books about the afterlife. She had also been watching over my health and recently sent me a lot of healing from spirit after I had a melanoma excised from my shoulder. A good example of how our loved ones in the afterlife still concern themselves in our daily lives on earth.

Judy confirmed that my earlier full-time career roles as a radio and TV presenter were actually essential as training for the more important task now at hand. Judy referred to my past-life research, which is an integral part of this book, of which Ezio was completely unaware. Judy confirmed that she, too, had played a key role in the past lives that we had shared. She referred to a life that we had had in France several hundred years ago, saying that her appearance then was very similar to what it had been in her last life, only she was "much stockier."

A year before meeting Judy in this life I had been in France to report on the Cannes Film Festival in 1992, and, more important, had two past-life experiences while I was there. The festival was like a garish circus and I couldn't wait to escape the madding crowds and go exploring.

My first experience was in the mountain town of Tourrettes-sur-Loup in Provence, where I was shown a vision of myself working as a nun in the small church. When I went inside I felt very familiar with the church, although the layout did not feel quite right. I tuned in and was shown a vision of it before it was rebuilt after being destroyed in the religious wars. My vision showed that the original nave was in a completely different position to that of the present building. I was puzzled by this, but an expert from the local tourist office who had seen drawings of the old church confirmed it was true. In my vision I saw myself working in the gardens of the church, cultivating herbs and vegetables.

My second experience occurred a week later in the medieval city of Guérande in Brittany. My spirit guide came into my thoughts while I was traveling from Carcassonne to Paris by train, and told me to get off at the next stop, which I did with complete trust. As the train pulled into the next station I saw my unscheduled stop was St. Nazaire, a port town at the mouth of the Loire River. I got off the train, wondering what my next move would be and decided to get a taxi and asked the driver to take me to a seaside hotel.

My French-language skills were obviously lacking that day, and he deposited me outside a hotel on the docks area of the waterfront. I was bemused when I looked around, but, feeling there was a reason for all this, I booked into what turned out to be a fairly run-down hotel. It was hardly surprising that I was the only guest in what was a popular watering hole for the waterfront workers. But my trust in my guide paid off when I met the delightful French owners, who seemed to understand my rudimentary French. Over the next few days I was made very welcome, and they even asked me to eat with them in their kitchen, where I remember watching a Clint Eastwood Western dubbed in French. It was a very unusual experience created by listening to and trusting my guide.

I hired a car and was guided along strange roads, trusting the spirit messages I was being given. After a while I saw a signpost to the medieval city of Guérande, which sounded too good to miss. I parked outside the walls and walked into the town center, where I had one of those amazing déjà vu experiences we only read about or see in films. I happily wandered around, feeling completely at home, being given a mind tour by my invisible guide. I went straight to the city center and the beautiful St. Aubin's Church, which my guide told me was the place where I had been married at around the time of the French Revolution. The church felt warm and inviting as I happily entered, and it felt good to know it had played a significant role in my past.

Both encounters had a deep impact on me at the time, far greater than the Cannes Film Festival. In retrospect, covering this event as a freelance broadcaster was undoubtedly only the catalyst for my going to France that year. As it turned out, being led back to Tourrettes-sur-Loup and Guérande for past-life glimpses was ultimately a far more important experience.

Judy unfortunately did not provide any details about the life we had shared in France, but instead referred to a connection we also had in "biblical times." Before I could inquire about either of these lives, she was joined in spirit by Rob, a mutual acquaintance who suddenly popped in to say hello. Rob was a bit of a larrikin in his life. Ezio described Rob's character to a T, and a few other details that cropped up during our session proved it was indeed the spirit of our friend. Unfortunately Rob's arrival broke the concentration surrounding the past lives Judy and I had shared, and I will have to wait for another occasion to explore them in detail.

After Rob breezed out Judy recalled that in the weeks leading up to her death she was heavily medicated and feeling disconnected. She remembered experiencing breathing difficulties and a burning sensation in her lungs and showed Ezio where the original condition started. Once again she was verifying everything that she was communicating, as Ezio, like Val Hood, had no idea about her medical history. Judy showed him a vision of her straddling a fence just before she died, demonstrating that she had a foot in both worlds at that time. She described the grass as being the same shade of green on both sides of the fence, indicating that she was not ready to pass over at that time.

As happens with many people in the last hours of their life, a group of souls started gathering around her, and Judy gradually realized it was time to go. One of those souls was that of a little boy, and Judy told us that he had died prematurely before she could give birth to him. Lying in her state of transition, she experienced a lot of remorse about losing him, which had happened many years before we met. While Judy said that she did not want to leave our relationship behind, especially as it took so long for us to reconnect, the presence of her unborn son made it a little easier for her to let go.

As I write these words I feel Judy's energy around me, along with that of my guide M. They let me know that the father of the boy is also now in spirit, and he and Judy have resolved the karma that brought them together briefly. He was a very troubled man who had a drug problem that destroyed his life and ultimately caused his death. M tells me that he has been receiving a lot of help in the afterlife, but will have to go back to earth to resolve his addiction in another life.

Judy remembers looking around the congregation at her funeral service and noting that people had come from far and wide to bid farewell to her. When it was time to cross over after the funeral, a friendly man came to assure her to "come across, you won't regret it," and that was the moment she let go of her earthly connection.

Judy told us that the man's name who put her at ease was Bill, and she identified him as one of my relatives. I knew immediately that she was referring to my father, who had passed over some twelve years prior to Judy. They had never met before this.

Judy went on to say that she felt great sorrow at first for leaving, but then great euphoria at what was coming up for her. Confused at first about the man who had met her, she then looked at him and recognized part of me in him. Bill told Judy that he wanted to be there for her to do a favor for me. Judy said she realized Bill was there to meet her, because "he knew what the big plan was."

She later found out that Bill works as a kind of guide in the afterlife, helping certain people cross over to the other side. He performs what Judy describes as a meet-and-greet service wherever appropriate. Although most people are met by a relative or close friend, for a variety of reasons some souls have nobody to greet them, and this is where Bill and his fellow guides step in. He apparently also coordinates the meet-and-greet for all members of his extended soul group, which is why he was there for Judy.

This was very interesting for me, as I had been told in a reading many years before meeting Judy that my father was working as a guide. I found this strange, given his lack of spiritual interest during his life. I had presumed that he must be working as a spirit guide and is an advanced soul, after all. Once I learned about his special guide duties for those spirits crossing over, it all made perfect sense. It was, in Ezio's words, another anchor thrown out to me from the afterlife. It was also interesting that Bill and Ernie, who got along well with each other on earth, were now working together in spirit.

When Judy crossed over, Bill organized a welcome-home party for her, a table laden with seafood of all descriptions. Even though spirits do not need to eat or drink once they have settled back into the afterlife, it is customary to welcome a returning soul with some kind of celebration. Ezio was not to know that my father was a great lover of prawns and oysters in his last life, as indeed was Judy, so it was not surprising that he would create a seafood feast for her. Many familiar spirits were gathered at the welcome-home party, helping her to adjust to her new surroundings. Judy described the event as happy and up-lifting for her, despite feeling a little melancholy, knowing it would be a long time before she would once again be with family and friends from her last earth life.

Judy let me know that my father will also be there to greet other members of my family, and one of his prime tasks will be to help them realize they are not "dead." Ezio felt that Bill did not believe in the afterlife when he passed, and this made him ideal for his cur-rent job. Judy described her special "meeter and greeter" as putting her completely at ease, and she soon realized that "it was not the end." After the celebration dinner Bill took her to another part of the Heaven World to visit Mary, an aunt who had passed over many years before.

Bill suddenly joined in the conversation and mentioned he will give special attention to John when he crosses. When Ezio asked if I knew who John is, I knew immediately that Bill was speaking about his brother-in-law, who is now in a nursing home, gently drifting away with dementia. Bill and John were great mates, having both worked at the same bank and shared similar values. John supervised Bill's estate when he died, and now Bill will return the favor when he eventually welcomes home my mother's baby brother. Her sister, who is in the same nursing home, will also enjoy Bill's meet-and-greet service. M tells me Bill will also be there at the gate when I eventually transition, which is a comforting thought.

My father was a very conservative man in life, an old-fashioned bank manager, who helped many people. He has apparently carried over that dignity to the afterlife as he goes about his guide duties. I was also gratified to learn that while we had never been as close as I would have liked, he is now a strong supporter of the work we are all doing to bring our two worlds closer together. At last I am able to feel a growing bond between us.

To wrap up the story of her crossing over, Judy threw us another anchor when she brought up the name Ultimo, and showed Ezio a vision of this inner-city Sydney neighborhood where we had lived together. Just before her passing, Judy and I had bought an investment property in Ultimo and I kept her informed as to how it was being renovated when she became too ill to leave her bed to see it for herself. It meant a lot to her at the time and she enjoyed hearing the stories about its refurbishment. There was a lot more to the story of the Ultimo property, which unfolded after she passed away, and once again Judy was sending me a special message confirming she knew about later events.

41

Healing Past Wounds

Many people believe that once we cross over to the afterlife we are magically cured of any health problems that may have plagued our physical body, and everything is suddenly wonderful.

Looking at my own experience from my last life as Brian, the young soldier who died in the Great War, I recall being taken to a healing center, much like a hospital. Here I was nursed back to full health with several "baths,"[1] where I was surrounded by a soft, violet-colored light. Some form of healing is essential for everyone when we first cross over, as the spirit still bears the imprint of the life just lived, even though the physical body has been discarded.

However, each afterlife experience is unique, and Judy tells a slightly different story of the events surrounding her crossing over into the world of spirit. Initially she says she was a little bit scared, but Bill's kind words encouraged her. Drifting in and out of both worlds just before she passed also gave her a sense of confidence.

When she finally crossed over she was quickly able to leave her body behind, together with all its physical ailments. At first she expected to be taken to some kind of place similar to the hospital in which she died, but Bill just laughed as he told her that was not the way it was going to work for her. At this stage she started to experience a "great sense of warmth inside" and then felt that her physical parts had been washed away fairly quickly. But there were other parts of her life experiences that proved much harder to clear, and these were dealt with at a later stage as part of her life review. Judy described these as "soul scars that had been there for a long time." These scars proved to be the hardest to leave behind and involved imprints from past lives as well as the life she had just completed.

At first Judy thought that she had dealt with and completed her issues during this last incarnation, particularly as she and I had been able to connect for a short but deep and loving relationship. However, after her initial healing she realized that certain scars in her spirit were profoundly embedded and were more intense than the physical problems that she had suffered. Any imprint that was left on her spirit from her physical ailments seemed to diminish pretty quickly, but imprints left from emotional scars earlier in life took longer to fade.

Any emotional problems that we brush aside or bury deeply in our lives usually stay with us as an impression on our spirit energy, and need to be addressed and healed in the afterlife. Brian had been nursed back to health after his wartime horrors and described some loving souls who stood around his bed, sending him loving energy without saying a word. Judy spoke of several angelic beings who came to help her. One she described as bearded and appeared "rather Jesus like," adding that it wasn't actually Jesus, just a look-alike. The "angel" told Judy all she had to do to heal herself was to wish it away; she no longer had to carry around all that "stuff" from her previous life. The angel emphasized the importance of accepting that in the world of spirit you are no longer the person you left behind. She then realized how simple it was—all she had to do was release her responsibility from any negative attachments so that she could move on unencumbered to the next stage of her new life.

Healing is a matter of time, but it is sometimes also a matter of opportunity.

—HIPPOCRATES, 460–370 BCE,
Greek physician

42

Judy's Life Review

When we have been through the healing process, the next step is usually a meeting with the Council of Elders, at which we are taken back through our previous life to review the events in a gentle and loving way. Each lifetime is part of a learning experience, and at the start of each new incarnation we agree to set a series of goals. Like a post-match sporting review with the coach, meeting the Council is the time for an open and honest appraisal of our efforts.

The number of councillors varies for each person, and Judy said three members greeted her in a very casual and laid-back outdoor setting. She had been accompanied there by the spirit of her aunt Mary, whom she had met again after the welcome-home seafood dinner. Judy said she was feeling "displaced" after completing her healing, and Mary stepped in and virtually adopted her, together with Judy's spirit guide. The "Jesus look-alike" angel turned out to be her spirit guide, whom she referred to as Nathan.

Aunt Mary and Nathan stood off to one side as Judy met with the Council, but assured her they were there if she needed support. The Elders chose to present themselves in white robes, and the leader of the group looked to Judy like an archetypal ancient philosopher, complete with long white beard. She found them to be very kind and helpful as she looked at her life in a series of flashbacks. While there were several unresolved emotional issues that still needed attention, overall they were pleased with the way she had lived her life. They also informed Judy that she would now be able to advance in the spirit world without having to return to earth for another lifetime if she so chose. Judy was delighted at this news as she was feeling very worldweary. The Elders told Judy she would have many new duties allocated to her once she had completely healed and settled into her new surroundings. They also informed her there is the potential for her to be born into another world at some stage.

You seek help from the elders. A society with elders is healthy. It's not always that way in the West.

—BERNARD LAGAT,
champion athlete

Following her life review, Judy knew she could totally release herself from being responsible for this life any longer. There were still lessons to be embraced and she would be able to see this life in the context of all her past lives and finally understand the progression of her soul experiences. The one thread that linked all her lives was her soul family connections. She described this link as tentacles that went in many different directions, connecting with all the people she had been associated with through the ages.

Judy mentioned a person who had caused her a lot of emotional grief in her last life, which had been a prime cause of the scars that had embedded themselves on her psyche. She discovered that he was linked to her soul group, and the relationship was in fact karmic, and needed to be played out in this emotional way for the benefit of both their souls. This realization came as something of a surprise to Judy after she was shown the evidence in her review.

As Judy looked back over some of her past lives she saw connections between us going back to Roman times, also around the times of the legendary King Arthur in Britain, as well as the life we shared in France in the Middle Ages. In at least one of these lives Judy saw herself as a very fiery male warrior, with a feisty, protective demeanor that she had built up, and persisted through to her very last life on earth. The fact that she was a warrior in a previous life came as a shock to Judy as she believed that she "never had it in her" to do this.

As Judy looked back over her previous lives, she felt a sense of discomfort as she once again saw some of the events in which she had participated. This proved to her that we can never really completely walk away from our past, as it shapes who we are today.

For no apparent reason Judy showed Ezio a vision of a national park in the suburb of Lane Cove in Sydney. She identified the park by name, which baffled me at the time. A few days later it suddenly hit me like the proverbial ton of bricks. Judy's body was buried in the neighboring cemetery, which overlooks this national park. This was another anchor to verify the information she was providing.

43

∞

Our First Meeting

By all accounts Judy is a very active spirit, reflecting the energy she displayed in her last life. We were together in this lifetime for a period of only four years, but they were packed with many experiences, and we managed to fit a lot into such a short period of time. I was working in a freelance capacity as a broadcaster and lecturer in radio journalism, so fortunately we were able to spend a lot of time together. When I thought about it after she passed, I realized we spent as much time together in four years as most people in a relationship would in ten.

Our meeting was obviously part of our destiny, arranged while we were still in spirit. We were seated two guests apart at a birthday dinner for Judy's friend, who had introduced us a couple of weeks beforehand. Judy suddenly turned and looked at me intensely and our eyes locked. She later confided that at that moment she realized that she would spend the rest of her life with me. Her premonition turned out to be chillingly accurate. After our first date I, too, realized this was not going to be just an affair of the heart.

I was booked to travel to Europe a few weeks later, to link up with my daughter, and Judy suddenly decided that she would join us a few days after that in Barcelona. The three of us had some great adventures traveling through Spain, Portugal, France, and Italy. One memory etched in my mind was the night we arrived by train in Rome. We had no accommodation booked there, or anywhere else we visited, preferring to trust to fortune. We found a hotel through the rail station information desk and went to get a taxi. There were none in sight, so an elderly man with a handcart told us he would take our luggage to the hotel and we could follow behind. There are some dodgy characters around train stations in Europe, but we figured at his age we wouldn't have a problem.

But without warning this elderly porter took off like a rabbit, pulling his handcart with all of our luggage onboard, heading off into the night. Not having a clue where we were heading, all we could do was run along behind him like a gaggle of geese. Fortunately the hotel was only a few blocks away, and we arrived out of breath and laughing like a bunch of schoolkids. He looked at us like we were crazy, as this was obviously his normal modus operandi. As they say, "When in Rome . . ."

When we returned home, Judy and I naturally started living together. There was never a dull moment in the next four years. We lived in four different houses and purchased two others together as investments, and were with each other virtually every day until she passed away. Even though I was working part-time and she was running a business from home, we also shared a love of the spiritual, and appeared as a team at several psychic events.

Six months before Judy passed we started a spiritual radio program, *Celestial Power*, broadcasting each Sunday from her home. Afterward I felt I had to move out of her house, which resonated with its memories of her last days, and headed for a beachside suburb where I set up my little studio. My son Matthew suggested it was time for a new name for the program, and came up with *Radio Out There*. The program is still on air today and is broadcast on the Internet to a worldwide audience.

It was a matter of course that Judy eventually came to me in a dream contact, proudly showing me the rose-covered cottage where she lived in the world of spirit. It was the kind of property we had often spoken about buying together in the mountains.

44

Working with Skeptics

As the session with Ezio progressed, Judy talked about having animals around her house in spirit, and expressed a love of nature, in what she calls "the Heaven World." This term for the afterlife was new to both Ezio and me, and the simplicity of it appealed.

When I asked Judy what she was doing now, her reply made Ezio chuckle: "I can't believe you just said that, I'm working with you, of course." This was a typical Judy retort, where I was put firmly in my place. She then laughed and added that her work now is to help create this book as part of our soul partnership. Judy also confirmed that she is one of the spirits working on John Dingwall's team. Apparently the group comprises more than ninety spirits, so it is no wonder they are able to provide so much detail about life in their world. Judy said the same thing as John: that they wish to get as much information to me as possible before I am too old to write, or before I pass over. She hastily added that this will not happen for quite some time, which brought a smile to my lips. It also made me wonder, how much information is still forthcoming?

Not to be put off, I persisted and asked her, "Surely you're not working with me all day, every day?" So Judy, like any other busy woman, listed in detail her main activities in the afterlife.

The book is her first priority, and she also played an important part inspiring me to write my previous book, *Afterlife*. Judy confirmed that this is actually "part of the blueprint" for both of us, created when we came together in her last life. We are now working jointly to get this information out to as many people as possible. Shortly after she returned to the afterlife, Judy realized that this was part of our destiny, and this explained why she pushed so hard for so many years to get me started on writing. I kept receiving messages from various mediums telling me it was about time I started writing a book—one message came from my friend Bob Murray, a medium who lives in Canada. However, I am a great believer in things happening when the time is right, so I don't feel too guilty about it.

Judy started to talk about some of her other activities. I had earlier discovered through her contact via Val Hood that she was working with children, but just as she was in life, Judy is now a very busy spirit in the afterlife. I remember her as being very independent in many ways, and she believed that people need to take responsibility for themselves and their actions. Judy admitted she now accepts that occasionally she lacked a little compassion because of this strong conviction. There were times when she saw that people needed help, but she stood back, thinking they needed to work hard to change their circumstances to solve their problems themselves. Some people did change, but a lot of others just made excuses not to do anything. This made Judy wonder whether she had been too hard on some people.

Being a highly focused archetypal Scorpio in her last life, Judy wondered why, if she could take control of herself, other people couldn't do the same. I remembered when she firmly made up her mind to quit smoking after several token attempts; she just gave it up "cold turkey" then and there, and never smoked another cigarette. Unfortunately it was too late to save her life. The issues around control are just one of the areas she has been working on in her ongoing group sessions in the afterlife.

Judy admitted that when she passed she was confronted by the issue of control and had to learn how to have more compassion. She referred to the kind of compassion shown to her by my father, Bill, as he helped her to cross over. That simple little act was enough to open her mind to how people need help to understand and come to terms with certain things.

Judy mentioned that I, too, have a strong attitude about people taking responsibility for their actions. I realized when I heard this that Judy has definitely been working closely with me, as this has become one of my focuses in the last few years. People who prefer to "pass the buck" rather than face their responsibilities are very frustrating to me.

One of Judy's other jobs in the afterlife is based around this issue of personal responsibility. She employs her newfound compassion working with new souls arriving in the afterlife, helping them to become more self-reliant in their next life, and not just depend on government handouts or on other people's generosity. Judy spoke of the concepts she has learned in the afterlife that can help people on earth create more rewarding lives, by understanding that their circumstances, difficult and challenging as they may be, are an important part of their development. We can learn our greatest lessons in times of adversity. It is vital that people accept responsibility for their actions so that they can learn their lesson and move on.

The other passions Judy explores in the afterlife revolve around communication. She is helping train certain negative spirits that have crossed over so that they will be able to work positively with their family and close friends back on earth. An important part of this work is dealing with skepticism about life after death. She is working with former closed-minded skeptics, whom Judy described as not believing in the afterlife and "the hierarchy of angels" during their previous life. Eventually, after realizing that life is a continuing process, they will be sent back in spirit form to break down the barriers they helped erect when they were previously on earth. This education program demonstrates how people in spirit can come back and help us, if we choose to take heed of their messages.

Those skeptics who believe there is nothing to look forward to but blackness after they die do not realize that they create that very experience for themselves when they first leave the body. When they finally accept help from more advanced spirits, they discover how wrong they were, and the blackness around them fades away. The education process that Judy works with helps these skeptics realize the potential damage they have created in their last life, and, most important, trains them to do something about it.

I was delighted to hear Judy say that she has enjoyed a lot of success in her project to remove this skepticism about the afterlife. I avoid cynics with closed minds as much as possible, because over the years I have seen what mischief they can create around vulnerable people. No amount of discussion or evidence will convince them to open their minds.

Once Judy and her colleagues have worked with these reformed spirits, they are instructed to go back and give their loved ones a real sign that they are still around. Sometimes these signs can be conveyed by a message from a medium, but in many cases they occur as something "mysterious or otherworldly" to get the point across. This can be anything from a dream or a voice in the stillness of the night to a book falling off a shelf with an appropriate message, or even an appearance in spirit form. Some spirits are informed that they may also have to continue this work in their next life if they have caused widespread fear or ignorance. It is part of an ongoing process by the spirit world to remove the doubt from as many skeptical minds as possible. This will, of course, be to their ultimate benefit when these reformed spirits next return to the afterlife and are able to avoid another sojourn in the black closet they have created.

A quirky thought crossed my mind: As there seems to be an

upsurge in the number of mediums now, it would be fascinating to know how many of them were closed-minded skeptics in a past life. My guide M provided this insight and confirmed that I, too, had been one in a past life! Another little piece of my karma exposed.

Judy told Ezio, much to his amazement, that she had also been part of the group working with TJ, a young man in spirit with whom Ezio is in regular contact. TJ's fascinating story is an integral part of Ezio's book, which he wrote with his wife, Michelle, *Postcards from the Other Side.* Spirit truly works in mysterious ways.

Judy then spoke about a former skeptic named George, who has now become her protégé in the Heaven World. George was sent back to respond to a call from his family to give them a sign that he was now happily living in the afterlife. George answered their request for survival evidence by making a pile of pots and pans fall off a rack on the wall. His family got the message.

The remaining part of her work in the afterlife Judy dismissed as "simply admin." In other words, all the work behind the scenes necessary to make these changes happen. Judy says she really enjoys this side of her work, especially when she sees the message get through to somebody who didn't believe that life continues after we leave our body. Acceptance of survival not only helps doubters on earth but makes it easier on their loved ones in the afterlife.

Judy still keeps an eye on her family from her previous life and, despite some emotional problems that occurred in her last couple of years, surrounds them with love from her place in the afterlife. Judy referred to a client who had "ripped her off badly" in a business deal, creating a financial hassle for her. She had to come to terms with it as part of her healing in the afterlife and was told to forgive and forget. At first she found it hard to forgive him, but was eventually able to put it all into context as a role that person played in her life's lessons. Being able to forgive and move on has made her advancement easier in the afterlife. Judy described this as the hurt of the action that leaves an imprint on the soul, and must be cleared.

Describing the two of us as twin flames, Judy once again mentioned that our relationship on earth was predestined, defining it as "diverging, converging, and then diverging again." I can only suppose she was referring to our entire life story, as we both reincarnated just three years apart in the same city, coming together again only in the last four years of her life. Parting after such a short time together was very distressing for both of us, but Judy says that is what the pain of grief is all about. Grief takes us through emotions that we would not otherwise experience or even recognize. She explained how the emotions and pain that we suffer in grief will eventually go on to become part of our life review in spirit. She described it as a "processed cleansing" similar to the pre-operation procedure carried out in the hospital before we go into surgery.

The life review process actually started for Judy when she was bedridden before crossing over, with a lot of hallucinations and visions. Some of these visions she remembers as cloudy and confused, but she later found their true meaning. This life review process continued for her after she went back to spirit. It became part of her healing process, which happened almost straightaway with a light that penetrated inside her.

Judy's story of her passing and crossing into the afterlife differed greatly from the experience I recalled from my previous life, and highlights the fact that everyone's transition experience is unique. Just as in life on earth, no two stories are the same, supporting the concept, "As above, so below."

Our life is what our thoughts make it.

—MARCUS AURELIUS, 121–180 CE,
Roman emperor

Part Five

More from the Afterlife Team

45

⚬

Contact Deepens

Now that I knew a little more about the group that supported John, which was made up of more than ninety spirits, including Judy and my father, I was eager to reestablish contact with them after a few months' break.

We changed our modus operandi slightly when Kelly decided to take John's advice from spirit and go into trance the evening following the group meditation sessions at the Australian Casa at his property, Eagles Nest. These meditations are known as "current," by which the participants are able to link and raise their energies to facilitate spiritual healing. This is done in concert with John of God's Casa in Brazil, where doctors in spirit come through to help thousands of people each week with healing. The residual energy from that day's current was able to help Kelly as he went into trance in an adjoining room of the Casa.

When Kelly, in deep trance, allows his spirit to rest quietly in a corner, John's energy is able to enter his body and make use of its physical attributes. Kelly's voice changes and becomes that of his father. The vocal tones, pace, and phrasing are completely different from Kelly's. John's signature is his distinct chuckle when he has integrated with Kelly and his voice, soft at first, soon becomes stronger as his spirit settles into his son's body.

Even though I had been champing at the bit to reestablish contact with John, Kelly's busy schedule had prevented this from happening for a few months. So by the time we connected again, I had a list of topics I wanted to discuss. John straightaway spoke about my impatience, revealing that the times of our contact had been chosen for us in spirit, and not the other way around, as I had supposed. As John said, "We like to think we have control of these things, but really there are greater forces organizing our connection."

John also needed his team to be available for him to establish contact, providing in each session their energy as well as their combined wisdom and experience. He said that teams such as his can number up to a thousand spirits, according to the situation at hand. When larger projects are being addressed, hundreds of thousands of spirits can be involved. He described these projects as "perhaps helping mankind with some of the greater things, such as injustices," which need a lot more energy.

So if John needs a backup team to be able to speak with us, albeit in trance, do other spirits need support when they communicate with loved ones on earth through mediums or other means? According to John, it is never just one spirit or one person, otherwise the connection would not be strong enough to last; it is always a team effort. "Even when people feel the energy of a spirit around them, it can be hundreds of people saying prayers, if you like, toward that connection." The mediums who tutored Anne and me at the Arthur Findlay College in the UK spoke of a control spirit that is always present, providing support as part of a contact, so we know that there are always at least two spirits working for each contact.

John went on to say that not only does it take a lot of energy for spirits to communicate with us but the conditions have to be right to make the appropriate connection. These situations are becoming more and more complex, what with the busy lifestyle of people on earth in the twenty-first century, as well as interference from technology. This is where the power of intention comes into play. If people make an appointment to see a medium or put themselves into the right conditions for communication, spirits are able to recognize the opportunity and act on it. However, intention alone does not always guarantee clear and concise contact, because outside factors over which there is no control sometimes interfere, which can be disappointing for everybody concerned.

Children can often see and communicate with spirits a lot easier than adults, but here, too, modern life is complicating matters. John was adamant that it's not like the 1950s, when children were told to go outside and play in the fresh air; now they are more likely to stay indoors and sit with electronic devices. Young people's minds are also being clouded by more and more fear being programmed into them by society, creating a barrier to spiritual communication. John was referring to stories of violence reported every day by the news media, as well as what many people recognize as the overprotective strictures of an increasingly litigious society.

In general, spirits are not just allowed to slip down to earth to communicate with people however and whenever they feel like it. John maintains that God is the only one who does not need some kind of permission to communicate with people on earth. Everyone else needs to get clearance from the appropriate source, usually guides or perhaps from one of the many "committees" that oversee this. There are rules in the spirit world that have to be observed by everyone, but there is always someone on hand to be of help when it's needed. "There has to be an order for things to work, that's important," John said. It is also essential for contact to be made when the time is right for all concerned.

John mentioned that he, in turn, was part of the support group for Judy when she communicated with me through Ezio De Angelis. Spirits are often asked to put their energy toward a communication without even knowing the other people involved. Their role is simply to concentrate on providing energy as part of a meditation to help that connection. They do not take part in, or are not aware of, any of the information being passed on, because it is private and none of their concern. John described this form of meditation as being very powerful and capable of being refined and turned into many things, such as a healing or even "something like time travel." (This is a concept that has always fascinated me, and I made a mental note to pursue the question of time travel in a future contact.)

The same situation applies at John of God's center in Brazil when Medium João allows spirit doctors to work through him while he is in trance. In each session, hundreds and hundreds of people meditate in "current" to create the energy for the spirit doctors to provide many forms of spiritual healing. The people meditating have no idea which one of the thirty-three doctors in spirit is on duty in that session, or what information or healing is being passed on. They are simply providing support energy. However, at the same time they themselves are also receiving some of the healing energy from Spirit.

In general, everyone in the afterlife and also on earth has a "cluster of spirits" supporting and working with them, according to John, in order to better that person's life.

Again, as above, so below.

46

Unconditional Love and Unresolved Emotions

Life in the Heaven World opens up so many exciting areas to explore each time we return. The power of thought creation, the idea of other worlds, future possibilities for our next incarnation, and the ability to learn and develop spiritually from our mistakes are just a few of the opportunities available. As I prepared for our next session with John and "Team Spirit," the whole question of relationships came to mind. From the many readings I have given over the years, it is obvious that problems and emotions concerning relationships are things that affect most people. My theory is relationship issues are part of a generational karma, especially for those born in the last half of the twentieth century, and I wondered if there were similar problems in the afterlife. How do spirits relate to each other: Is it all love and light? Is unconditional love a universal practice in the Heaven World?

Not a lot changes when you return to the spirit world, according to John. Humans like to think there is such a thing as unconditional love, but whether we like it or not, people put conditions around love. This is an area where spirits learn a lot of lessons, as it cuts through to the very heart of who we are. Unconditional love is one of the most powerful emotions we can pursue, and this can open up a lot of negativity in people on earth. It means loving with no rules and expecting nothing in return, which is very difficult in such a material world.

So when spirits return to the afterlife they bring these unresolved emotions with them. Old enemies do not suddenly put their arms around each other in a loving hug, divorced couples may still detest each other, and for a lot of people all is not instant bliss and harmony. This becomes part of the work they must do in the afterlife, to understand and release these negative emotions that are restricting their soul growth. While spirits are working through these issues and also preparing for the next life, new emotions may often arise. John said that he does not see all the spirits in his environment "rolling around with a loving heart, or having love-ins." Spirits still retain their personality, but once they are able to work through their emotional problems, they can advance to higher planes.

John explained that spirits from these higher levels are easily distinguishable because you can feel the intense love energy they project. "You can have a spirit move past you, and the feeling of pure love emanating from them may bowl you over and just leave you stunned, with no words spoken." John recalls having experienced many higher spirits in his energy field, sometimes for only a fleeting moment, and said that he felt humbled by that experience. Like everyone else, he is still striving to be a better person in relationship to others.

Important emotional issues that spirits work with in their soul groups include guilt, egotism, and forgiveness. It is vital to understand and come to terms with the situations that caused such great disharmony in their recent life. Until all the reasons for conflict are analyzed and understood, spirits are unable to move on to the next stage of their development, whether it is in the afterlife or in their next incarnation. The other members of the group are also learning and advancing by association, in what is really a spiritual classroom. This sometimes means a spirit will find it important to get a message to someone on earth, asking for their forgiveness. It is never too late to practice forgiveness, in either this world or the next; it works both ways.

Psychologist Dr. Stephanie Sarkis writes:

> Forgiving doesn't mean forgetting, nor does it mean that you've given the message that what someone did was okay. It just means that you've let go of the anger or guilt toward someone, or toward yourself. But that can be easier said than done. If forgiveness was easy, everyone would be doing it.[1]

However, it came as a surprise for me to learn that nobody is actually forced to attend these group sessions to clear the past and move on. There are spirits who, according to John, live in almost a dark limbo and refuse to participate and learn their lessons. They then return to earth in their next incarnation no further advanced than when they were last there, and have to experience the same negative conditions all over again. The concept of free will applies in the spirit world as well as on earth.

> *The weak can never forgive. Forgiveness is the attribute of the strong.*

> —MOHANDAS K. GANDHI, 1869–1948

Many people find it hard to grasp the concept of a world of spirit. Kelly had been asked by a friend who was looking for a simple, basic explanation of the main difference between what he described as "here and there." He wanted to know what he was going to be "up for" when he eventually leaves this world. John summed it up with his unique sense of humor, saying the first thing to tell this man is that in the afterlife he will save on food bills! On a more serious note, the main difference is that, overall, life in spirit is easier, because, for a start, there is no physical body, with its needs and ailments, to worry about; nor are there the issues surrounding money, which creates a lot of stress and illness. In short, there are none of the negative demands of everyday life on earth. A simple explanation of the spirit world is not easy to come up with, but John, who by now was getting into journalist mode, expanded his definition of the afterlife as a place where we go to learn about ourselves, and also to rest in between lives.

He went on to talk about the problem of the simplistic attitude that is fostered in so many people that after they die they're going to either somewhere good or somewhere bad. Deep down, the vast majority of people know they have done something in life to feel guilty or remorseful about. No matter who these people are, or what their standing in life, they will still wonder whether they're going to end up in the bad place. While Spirit tells us there is no such place as hell, there are areas of the afterlife that John described as "an institution where certain spirits are sent to learn."

To summarize, John suggested that Kelly tell his friend that what happens in the afterlife depends on what you do right now. This rang true for me, as I have been contacted by many people who have read *Afterlife* to say that the information in the book has had a big influence on the way they decide to live their life now, and they have resolved to make the necessary changes to be better people.

As usual, John had the final word on the subject: "If you knew you were going to live somewhere else, and your current life would be looked at under a microscope, with your actions determining the kind of life you will have there, wouldn't you want to take a good, hard look at yourself?"

> *Success is to be measured not so much by the position that*
> *one has reached in life as by the obstacles which he has*
> *overcome while trying to succeed.*

> —BOOKER T. WASHINGTON, 1856–1915,
> educator

47

Genetic Modification Concerns

The mass development of genetically modified crops risks causing the world's worst environmental disaster.

—HRH THE PRINCE OF WALES,
interview, *Daily Telegraph*, August 12, 2008

The question of genetic modification (GM) is ringing alarm bells for many people all over the world. Also known as genetic engineering, the techniques have been applied in numerous fields, including research, agriculture, industrial biotechnology, and medicine. Just before connecting with John and his group for another session, a newspaper story caught my attention: Scientists are experimenting with the DNA from three different parents to produce a child who will be potentially free from certain health problems. My intuitive alarm system went into hyperdrive. Genetically modified food crops and cloning are already very controversial subjects on earth, but what do they think in the afterlife?

I wasn't surprised to learn that spirits in the afterlife share our concern for the future of life on earth. John's group's reaction was immediate, describing the whole GM movement as "one of the scariest topics of conversation in the spirit world." There is apparently "huge concern" in the afterlife that humans are advancing too quickly in this area of scientific modification for both food and the human condition. "They're advancing faster than they really have the knowledge for creating small breakthroughs, and instead of consolidating this knowledge over many years, they are giving in to the desire for instant gratification." The testing that does happen is far too minor for the end result to be completely positive.

> *The cloning of humans is on most of the lists of things*
> *to worry about from science, along with behavior control,*
> *genetic engineering, transplanted heads, computer poetry,*
> *and the unrestrained growth of plastic flowers.*
>
> —LEWIS THOMAS, 1913–1993,
> physician, poet, etymologist, essayist

The feeling in the spirit world is that the altering of human DNA has dire consequences for the future. John says it is being created by scientists and drug companies who are "after money and power."

Obviously, scientific research is essential for improving our lives, otherwise such things as antibiotics, anesthetics, and many other medical breakthroughs would never have occurred, but in spirit they believe that this time we are going too far.

People on earth are busily striving for perfection in their lives, but this is not always what is really needed. These ambitions may also affect the flow of karma, because some people need to have a life in which they can surmount what may be regarded as impossible challenges. For example, this may be the case for a family whose karmic lessons involve looking after a child with a dysfunctional body. It would also apply to a family who wanted a child—a boy, for example—and manipulated the DNA accordingly. If the child had been intended to be a girl for her own soul experience, the modification could cause grave problems as the child grew up. John summed it up succinctly: "Just because people want something, doesn't mean that it is the best thing for them."

Eliminating one potential problem could well introduce unforeseen reactions. "There could be mutant strains of conditions that emerge, perhaps in the area of the brain that we don't know about," John said. This interference could have potentially explosive consequences in later life.

It can also affect generations yet to be born. The lessons that were supposed to be learned will not happen, or they will come in an entirely different and unpredictable form. It could also mean that the people involved may have to come back for another life to face the lessons they avoided.

"We do know that playing God when you are not God can be a bad thing," John said.

It is hard for us to know just how far we can take these experiments without stepping over the line. When I questioned whether this experimentation was part of the cause for the downfall of the ancient civilization of Atlantis, I was told there was nothing new about this kind of manipulation, which has happened many times in the past in several cultures.

On the question of genetically modifying food, John's group warned that there are dire consequences that may arise by "putting a rogue seed out there that could have the capability of wiping out a whole world of grain if we are not careful." John said that just as humans have been infected by viruses with deadly results, so does food have that capability of wiping itself out.

As giant corporations get more and more involved in the area of genetically modified food production, the advanced spirits in the afterlife who are able to look into the future describe this as being very dangerous. This would not be necessary if humans were eating properly and growing food as it was meant to be grown.

As for scientific research in other areas, there are developments that are being held back from common knowledge. In spirit, this is regarded as "not a bad thing," because the human race is not yet ready for some advances.

48

Accidents, Suicide,
Euthanasia, and Comas

There is always a lot of distress for families when loved ones die as
the result of an accident, during an operation, through violence, and
of course by suicide. Did they suffer, even for a few moments, especially when the death was sudden?

John was able to answer the question instantly when he told us
that the spirit leaves the body just prior to these distressing situations,
to prevent trauma from being imprinted on the soul. Our spirit usually stands to one side when we are going through an operation, leaving the body at the time the anesthetic is administered, once again to
ease the burden of trauma, which could leave a serious imprint on the

soul. Sometimes there is a jolt to the body just after the anesthetic is administered, particularly with children, as the soul leaves quickly. Other spirits then arrive to protect that soul while it is out of the body in an unfamiliar state.

However, if a spirit does not pass over immediately after an accident, or some similar incident, what happens in the intervening period may well be part of the experience that person agreed to in their life contract. Nothing happens by chance in these circumstances.

Sometimes people can remain in a coma for many months or even years before recovering, whether the coma is natural or medically induced. So what happens to the spirit while the body lies dormant? According to John, the spirit comes and goes from the afterlife as part of its growth experience. The spirit is often aware of its surroundings and the comings and goings of family and medical staff, and some of these memories are retained, but it is mainly back in the world of spirit, being nourished and supported while continuing its education.

The spirit also leaves just prior to the moment of death in a suicide. John had previously expressed his group's intention to discuss the whole question of suicide in today's society. I wrote in *Afterlife* that those who commit suicide are not punished but given special loving support to cope with the intense emotions surrounding them. Eventually, though, most of these spirits are sent back to earth to live another life and once again face up to the same conditions they attempted to escape previously.

In our latest session the group raised the topic of the concern felt in the afterlife about the growing numbers of people taking their own lives. Suicide is now at one of its highest levels ever, despite the so-called advancement in areas of medical knowledge, technology, and general lifestyle that many people enjoy, especially in Western countries. So another big question being addressed in the spirit world is, what can be done about the highest suicide rate in history?

The group emphasized that the forces that pressure many people to contemplate suicide have to be faced and conquered by all of us. These destructive influences range from medication, alcohol, and recreational drugs to many negative pressures that complicate our daily lives. There are even dark energies around us that interfere and create havoc. The "good spirits" that surround us are there to help and encourage. But ultimately it is up to the free will of the individual. As John said, there is no easy answer to this question.

Euthanasia is another question that creates a lot of controversy in a world wanting easy and instant solutions to its problems. It invokes strong emotions in people, as the proponents of euthanasia see themselves as fighting for their rights. They want to go out the way they choose in life, and families do not want to see their loved ones suffer. I have heard many people say that if you would euthanize a sick animal, why wouldn't you do the same thing for someone suffering from an incurable pain-filled illness?

Even in the afterlife, John said, euthanasia is a very "touchy subject" and is looked upon in a similar way to suicide, for a number of

reasons. Having the power of life and death can become very complicated, with the ultimate result that people may choose euthanasia not
for humanitarian reasons but because life is not going their way. It
could even lead to a form of population control in an increasingly
overcrowded world. The ramifications involved in legalizing euthanasia are creating great concerns in the spirit world.

Choosing euthanasia could also have a major impact on a people's
life contracts, as the pain they suffer was probably agreed to before
they were even born. "The last few months of someone's life could
well be when they have their greatest lessons," said John. This area of
medical research is regarded in the spirit world with as much concern
as IVF or genetic modification, particularly when power games are
employed. John gave the example of a couple having an IVF baby, but
deciding they only want a child of a certain sex. What happens if they
create "the wrong gender"?

However, the decision to switch off a life-support machine or stop
similar medication is regarded not as euthanasia but simply allowing
nature to take its course. John explained that by the time a decision of
this magnitude is made, everything possible has been done, and the
spirit has usually departed from the body, often several weeks prior.
The aura around the body would only be a gray mass. In many cases
this intervening period is necessary for the family to come to terms
with the situation and face their grief. John also said that sometimes
this is done deliberately so that the loved ones may use that time
when the person is on life support to start their healing process. Once
again, each case is unique.

Euthanasia is a long, smooth-sounding word, and it conceals its danger as long, smooth words do, but the danger is there, nevertheless.

—PEARL S. BUCK, 1892–1973,
awarded the Nobel Prize in Literature in 1938

The question of cryogenics also arose. The idea to cryopreserve humans started back in the 1960s, when Robert Ettinger, inspired by a science-fiction story, founded the Cryonics Institute in the United States. Inside the institute, more than a hundred bodies float inside giant bottles filled with nitrogen at temperatures of around minus 150 degrees Celsius. The hope is that one day in the future some doctor with advanced medical knowledge will revive them. One of the most famous names linked to cryopreservation is that of Walt Disney, who was very interested in the science. Although records show that Disney's body was cremated, great mystery surrounded his funeral, which was carried out in secret, and rumors persist that his body lies cryogenically frozen somewhere underground in Disneyland.

So if at some future time a medical advancement allows a body that was cryopreserved to be revived and physically healed, is it possible that person could come back to life? Would that same spirit, which had obviously returned to the afterlife, be able to return to its previous body? Would the spirit be able to choose to return, as in the case of someone in a coma, let alone be given permission by the Elders in the afterlife?

Many questions spring to mind about this whole bizarre concept, and most of us would probably dismiss it as pure science fiction. But, as we know, what we remember as yesterday's science fiction is coming true every day.

John used Walt Disney as an example: "Technically he would be able to come back, but he would not be Walt Disney anymore." This means that while Walt Disney's body might have been revived, it would give another spirit the opportunity to live in his body. The other point John raised was, who would be around to actually know it was Walt Disney?

Famous US TV presenter and interviewer Larry King announced to the world on the Larry King special *Dinner with the Kings* in 2011[1] that he wishes to be cryogenically preserved after his death. Born in 1933, Larry King was raised in the Jewish faith, but later declared he was agnostic.[2] During his very colorful life, King has risen to international stardom, conducted some 60,000 radio and TV interviews, including with some of the most famous people on the planet, and has so far been married eight times to seven different wives.

I have to wonder, when celebrities choose cryogenics, what unfinished business do they feel they still need more time to complete at the end of a long life? Perhaps it is the fear of death itself, or maybe it relates to the old saying that there are not too many people on their deathbed who tell their loved ones they wish they had spent more time at the office.

John Dingwall's group said that the technology of cryogenics could well be one of "the many medical breakthroughs that are just around the corner." He described medical science as being right on the cusp of important developments at the moment, but was not forthcoming with any details.

I guess we will just have to wait and watch.

49

Mental Health Conditions

There were several sensitive topics John's group wanted to address in future sessions, and as I went into the healing room, where Kelly was already fairly deep in trance, I had an open mind, wondering which subjects they would discuss that evening. John immediately set the tone of the session when he said there was a lot more about mental health the group wished to address, including how it affects people in both worlds.

The whole area of mental health is highly complex and perhaps more widespread than we would like to imagine. John's group had some potentially controversial points to make, describing mental health as a gray area, and people can often return to the spirit world with severe issues still deeply ingrained. The general feeling in spirit is that a lot of current mental conditions are connected with the nature of medication being prescribed. They believe the medication prescribed is not necessarily always about providing the people concerned with a better life, as is generally claimed. It is more about making life easier for those around them when mental outbreaks occur.

Certain medications often "slow down the healing process of that person and can actually prevent them from completely healing," John said. Mental health problems can be either part of a life contract or a combination of events that were created by the person concerned. John's example was that people who are "living on the edge" could have agreed to a life contract where they are to be given a choice of directions at a key point in their life. One direction will take them over the edge. This choice, which is part of the free will they are exercising, could involve such things as alcoholism, substance abuse, or extreme emotional situations, which would exacerbate the situation they are facing.

Whether mental illness is part of a life contract or a condition created during a person's lifetime, when each soul returns to the afterlife it carries an imprint on the spirit, which reflects the activities and emotions of that previous lifetime. This imprint can also be sitting on top of others, and may still be unresolved from different past lives. As previously discussed, each life contract we enter into contains karmic issues that must be addressed, but as our soul progresses through each incarnation, these imprints become less intense.

When spirits with mental health imprints finally return to the afterlife, they are sent to healing centers that specialize in these conditions, and they are helped there by teams of highly experienced spirits to deal with individual circumstances. John told us that an important part of his work is helping people with mental conditions, which explains his personal interest in this area. While he described these spirits as being damaged, John was quick to point out that everyone can be helped, it is just a matter of how long it takes each individual to heal.

Mental health problems can create a very deep imprint that is usually slower to heal than other medical conditions, and the healing period has a lot to do with the individual circumstances. This means there is naturally a longer process involved before that spirit is ready to reincarnate. Despite the work done in the afterlife, there can still be residual effects when that spirit does reincarnate, and these form part of the lessons it still needs to learn. We all bring back many hundreds of residual imprints into each incarnation that can manifest as problems and blockages that will need to be faced in that lifetime.

We all know that when things are difficult in life we tend to avoid them, because that is the easy way out. The hard thing is to tackle these problems head-on, but, according to advice from the afterlife, not many people choose to go that way. Many spirits actually ask for obstacles to be put into place before they reincarnate so that they will be given the opportunity to face up to their karma after having avoided these situations in previous lives. This can also include experiencing mental health problems.

These conditions are not easily swept under the rug; they have to be dealt with, and this impacts not only the person concerned but friends and other members of their family. So if these conditions have been agreed to, pre-incarnation, why is it so difficult for many people to resolve or even properly deal with their mental health problems?

John's answer was immediate. "One of the greatest obstacles in spirit's path in dealing with mental health issues is certain pharmaceutical institutions, which say they have miracle drugs that can cure problems. These include mental illness, as well as conditions such as depression and hyperactivity." He said that a lot of these lessons are placed there in spirit for a reason.

> *New ways of defining diseases, and educating people about the options for dealing with them, are urgently needed. To continue to rely on drug company–funded thought-leaders to write the definitions, and drug company–funded marketing to educate us about them, is dangerous, and really rather absurd.*
>
> —RAY MOYNIHAN AND ALAN CASSELS,
> *Selling Sickness*[1]

John went on to say that in the case of some children being born, whom he described as being ultrasensitive and often highly intelligent, the parents are the ones who have the most trouble dealing with them. "The parents are living in a society where they want to be entertained by all the visual aspects that are on offer. They don't have the patience or the environment to sit and spend the time with these children to help them." People are working too hard and come home too tired to cope with these children's special demands. It is easier to give them medication or some other form of distraction to make life easier.

John agreed that certain conditions have to be treated with medication, as they involve a chemical imbalance in the body. However, he affirmed that every case is individual. He made the point that medication is not always the ultimate answer, despite the fact that many people have placed sole reliance on this form of treatment.

Broadcaster and author Craig Hamilton wrote about the lifestyle changes that he found imperative in dealing with mental health problems. Craig spoke to me on *Radio Out There* about learning to live with bipolar disorder and is adamant that medication is only part of the answer. In his book *A Better Life*,[2] Craig tells how changing his diet, virtually giving up alcohol, and embracing such practices as yoga and meditation have all contributed to dealing with his illness. He acknowledges the importance of staying on his medication, but advocates an overall holistic approach. The big problem is that society still regards mental illness as something to be treated like a bout of the plague.

Complete peace equally reigns between two mental waves.

—SWAMI SIVANANDA SARASWATI, 1887–1963,
spiritual teacher and physician

"When someone is seen as being different, it often brings up fear in those people around them," said John. They are seen as needing treatment, and medication is the easy answer to "make them normal like us, in debt and stressed." Overall, people need to exercise great patience and understanding to help those with mental problems, especially the ones who cannot help themselves. John pointed out that it may also be in the life contract of those who are giving support to spend their lifetime in this way.

The tapestry of life weaves its own mysterious path for every one of us. Finding and following that path demands trust and an open heart.

50

Homosexuality

The issues of gay rights, gay marriage, and the like are so often in the news today, you would think that homosexuality had only been recently invented. Public opinions and attitudes are divided on this subject, and many fundamentalists are all too prepared to believe that gay people will go straight to hell when they die.

So what is the attitude in the afterlife to this delicate question?

"The love of one human being for another is not seen as a blasphemy," was the reaction from John's group. If two men or two women love each other, they are not punished in any way. The main consideration is the morals of the people concerned, something that applies to any relationship. The way people conduct their lives is what really matters, and the fact that they are homosexual is irrelevant.

The most important thing to remember is that we are all spiritual beings enjoying a human experience. John described homosexuality as simply expressing a sexual preference and nothing else. There is no spiritual law being broken and it is not considered immoral in the world of spirit.

There are so many qualities that make up a human being . . .
by the time I get through with all the things that I really
admire about people, what they do with their private parts
is probably so low on the list that it is irrelevant.

—PAUL NEWMAN, 1925–2008,
actor

Many people on earth are completely opposed to homosexual marriage, stating that any formal union must be between a man and a woman and is integral to the propagation of the species.

My heart beat a little faster when I heard the reaction from John's team: "If any individual truly opened their hearts to love, and felt the presence of true love, even for a few moments, they would not condemn anyone from loving another human being." What a beautiful sentiment, and surely something to be embraced in any relationship.

Once again it raised the question of life contracts, as certain relationships, homosexual or otherwise, can involve unresolved issues from past lives between the people concerned. A lot of complications arise between homosexual men and their fathers and between lesbians and their mothers, according to John, and these are highlighted because of the sexual situation. There may also be issues with the opposite sex that need to be faced and resolved in that lifetime.

When a person chooses to be a transvestite, it may also involve playing out past-life issues. If a spirit has had several past incarnations as the same gender, it can bring those strong senses back that may manifest in sexual preferences and appearance.

As part of his afterlife group studies into human nature and the tapestry of life, John has followed the lives of certain spirits over many incarnations. He likened this to reading a series of books about a certain person's lives, and spirits can spend weeks in a group session examining all the different scenarios and analyzing why these events unfolded as they did over many lifetimes. "It is a fascinating study of why and where things go wrong in life, and the reason we study it is so that we will not make those same mistakes."

Sometimes these studies involve historical figures, which, John said, makes it all the more interesting as a group analysis. Everything is examined and dissected, from the "ins and outs of their daily lives" to their relationships—why they failed and the strengths and weaknesses involved. Perhaps this could be classed as studying spiritual biographies.

51

The Dark Side

While Kelly is in deep trance, allowing John's spirit to take over his body and talk directly to us, he describes resting in a state of complete peace in a very quiet part of his being. Knowing that trance mediums are vulnerable at times like this, I asked John what protection measures were in place for Kelly. John informed us that "hundreds of spirits are here in the room with us, supporting Kelly." This is to prevent any dark spirits from taking advantage of the situation and jumping into Kelly's body to create mischief or even to take over.

It reminded me of the time several years ago when I was working with two mediums on live broadcast radio. We were taking calls and connecting listeners with their loved ones over the airwaves. When we listened back to a recording of the show the next day, it sounded as if we had a live audience on hand with so many spirits chattering away in the studio. The station manager couldn't believe his ears when he heard the playback on tape the next day, and we found a new believer!

John's support team has a twofold purpose, to provide Kelly with the energy needed to communicate clearly, and protect him at the same time. John emphasized the importance of putting in place correct protection for anyone connecting with the spirit world, casting aside the negatives generated by fear, and creating a barrier against negative spirits through the positive energy of love.

Lower or dark spirits are quite capable of entering and co-inhabiting a human body even if the person is not trying to connect with spirits. Usually there are other negative factors at work, such as drugs or alcohol, basically issuing an open invitation to these dark energies. It is also important to avoid treating contact with the spirit world as some kind of game, or using devices such as Ouija boards to conjure up spirits. In most cases, these pursuits are done with no protection at all and can be very dangerous, according to John, particularly if people are harboring negative thoughts at the time. It allows all kinds of spirits and entities access. There are also those people who are trying to access the spirit world for negative reasons, such as practitioners of black magic, and vulnerable people can easily become prey to dark entities at this time.

People who are "delusional or have mental problems are probably the worst persons to try to contact spirits," John said. Their minds are very vulnerable and they are opening themselves up to possession by dark energies ready and waiting to take over a physical body.

There are two main ways in which dark energy can take over the body. The most severe is *possession*, whereby a powerful and very low energy takes total control of the body at the connection point between the heart and the soul; here, they can exert a very powerful influence on that person through the emotions.

On the other hand, an *attachment* is less powerful than a possession. Attached spirits like to hang around and influence control over a person, but not necessarily inhabit them. These dark spirits are very clever, according to John, and the people concerned do not know they are losing control of their lives. These attachments also have the patience to hang around to trick their victims, and slowly work away to exert their influence. They know the weakness of the person concerned, such as ego, greed, or jealousy, and these entities have the knowledge and cunning to exploit this chink in their armor.

John emphasized a point he had made in an earlier session: the dark forces are stronger than those of the light. This means that, besides drugs, alcohol, and certain medications, the weaknesses around extreme negativity in a human can be exploited by a dark spirit to gain control. Negative emotions such as fear, hate, and anger can open the door for these entities.

If there is one thing I would banish from Earth, it is fear.

—HENRY FORD, *THEOSOPHIST* MAGAZINE, FEBRUARY 1930

Spirits working against the dark side do so from the heart; in other words, using the positive power of love. John's next words rang true:

"If you base yourself from the heart and work with it, you will never have a problem."

The dark spirits reside in the lower reaches of the afterlife as well as in other dimensions, and refuse to acknowledge the light. Many of them are still earthbound, clinging desperately to the places they were familiar with, refusing all offers of help to cross over to the world of spirit. Fortunately, this does not have to be a permanent state, as advanced spirits are working constantly to bring the light into these regions, and when a dark spirit is ready, it is able to move toward that light. However, this is a very slow process, and it takes a lot of energy to coerce them out of the void where they reside. It is a similar situation in many cases to the underworld these spirits inhabited in their previous life on earth.

It is important to bring these dark energies into the light, because their control over people on earth is interfering in the life contracts of those concerned, which can affect many more people in their environment. Dark energies continue the antisocial activities they indulged in before they died, with no respect for law and order. John said it is very difficult for the powers that be to control these spirits, because they can't just lock them away in some prison, as happens on earth. "They would exercise their free will and just walk through the walls!"

Spirits in the afterlife are also constantly working with the people on earth who have been possessed or have attachments, to help them release these dark energies. This often means working with experts on earth to help remove these entities, and the combined energy is often very successful.

Sonia, a spiritual healer who had helped clear my aura on a couple of occasions after I had been exposed to extremely negative situations, came to the rescue when a dark energy took up residence in my house. Sonia helped remove a family of spirits who had moved in and were causing great disruptions. They had taken over the area where my office was located and were blocking work opportunities from coming to me, as well as creating emotional disharmony in the household. A special clearing ceremony helped these interlopers to move on, and things started to improve almost immediately.

It was soon after this that I was introduced to the work of John of God; this marked a transformation point in my life, and eventually inspired me to write *Afterlife* in the very office that Sonia had spiritually cleared a couple of years earlier. It is always wonderful to realize and acknowledge our spiritual connections, and express gratitude for the help and guidance we are given from the Heaven World.

52

Prison Reform

There are many topics of discussion that I have brought up with John and his team over the many sessions we have had together, and I felt we had covered most major areas I needed for this book. So I was taken aback at the end of one session when they wanted to raise the subject of prisons in our next meeting. (Having just addressed the question of dark energies, I was intrigued to discover why John was so adamant about raising this topic.) The following week the team was obviously waiting impatiently to speak about prisons as John jumped straight in after our normal greetings, saying they wished to express their concern over the impact of these institutions. My reaction was, we have been locking people away for their misdemeanors all through earth's history, so why are spirits suddenly expressing such alarm?

I hadn't given any thought to the question of incarceration before this, and the group's answer proved to be obvious. Prisons are inhabited and controlled by dark spirits who make it nearly impossible for those from higher levels in the afterlife to intervene or have any positive influence. So there is little or no opportunity for Spirit to enlighten and heal those who are imprisoned. Extreme negativity is apparently present on a massive scale in these small areas.

John and his team described the whole prison situation as being another serious concern in the spirit world. They emphasized that it is an important issue in this day and age because of the increasing numbers of people being imprisoned, especially for drug-related crimes. This has a big impact on society as a whole, because prisoners are not being healed or rehabilitated but merely locked away and punished with an "out of sight, out of mind" attitude by the general public.

People in prisons are damaged individuals who need to be nurtured and healed, according to the team. The overwhelming view in the afterlife is that throwing people in prisons is "possibly the worst way of healing a human being imaginable."

If the system is not changed, "there are going to be dire consequences for the human race." The current system attracts the downfall of other humans with its inherent violence. It promotes negativity and the worst aspects of human nature. This negativity spreads within the walls of the prisons, and when these inmates are eventually released, they go back into the community and "spread their germs like a virus, which increases the problem tenfold."

These are times of high violence and the greatest use of illegal drugs and alcohol in history, which our team described as being at crisis point. The conclusion drawn in spirit is that the only things governments are doing is increasing the size and number of jails.

They wanted to make it clear that the urgent need is for internal change, and certainly not for the abolition of the prisons themselves. "Certain people still have to be kept away from society, but it is the environment in which they are held that is the most important thing." The feeling in the afterlife is that society cannot expect to lock people away, as we do now, treat them like wild animals, and then expect to release them back into the community without proper rehabilitation. For example, when pedophiles eventually return to the afterlife, they are treated with extreme caution, as they are on earth. John described pedophilia as an attack on the most vulnerable members of the community, virtually the actions of a bully. However, everything in the spirit world is a huge learning opportunity, and these spirits are placed in a special hospital environment. Although this is a separate area in the spirit world, it is not tantamount to being in jail. The emphasis is on healing and learning about the destructive path they led in their previous life.

Interestingly, these spirits are not forcibly detained in any way; as John pointed out, you can't chain up a spirit. However, they know they cannot advance to the next level until they have understood how their last life deviated from its purpose, and learned to rectify their behavior in future lives. (Recent media stories of pedophiles, particularly involving priests in many different countries, could easily be interpreted as an upsurge of pedophilia. Not so, according to those observing from the world of spirit. "There have always been pedophiles, but there has been a surge in the way it is being reported. The electronic media is now so instantaneous and voracious that we get to hear about it more often.")

The current attitude by authorities on earth is that when people are locked up, they will automatically learn their lesson. John equated this to a schoolteacher shutting a child in a room for an hour and then expecting that young person to have learned his or her lesson, something that rarely happens. The child is more likely to get angry and to rebel instead.

Given that "good spirits" cannot enter the prisons because they are virtually locked out, what is the solution?

Change has to start with those in control of the prison system. John maintained that if prisoners are given one-on-one guidance, together with nurturing, and are encouraged to practice things such as meditation, the problems would start to resolve. It comes down to the people in charge and the way the system is run. The changes needed are so widespread that a whole new structure will have to be put in place. However, the main problem is that governments will not make these changes because they are not politically expedient.

He who opens a school door, closes a prison.

—VICTOR HUGO, 1802–1885,
author of *Les Misérables*

A survey released by the BBC at the time of the writing of this book revealed that there were approximately nine million people held in prisons around the world, with half of them located in the United States, China, and Russia. In India, where meditation is a universally accepted practice in both the Hindu and Buddhist faiths, the number of prisoners—at 30 per 100,000 of total population, is the lowest percentage recorded in the world. Coincidence? Perhaps, but worth investigation.

In the prison system, everything is done for the easiest and most convenient path possible for those in authority, but ironically ends up costing the government more money in the long term. The other impediment to change in the prison system is the widespread community attitude that people need to be punished for their misdeeds, so why should we want to nurture them?

Spirits in the afterlife can identify these problems and express their concern, but it is still up to the world community to recognize the long-term benefits these changes will have and force governments to act. As the situation is worsening each year, it may take a new generation of reformers, perhaps recently born or even yet to reincarnate, to provide that inspiration.

53

TV in the Afterlife

Several subjects popped up from time to time in the many sessions we had with John and his spirit team. Some of this information produced a laugh, or even an unexpected revelation about our life on the other side.

On one occasion John casually mentioned something about people in the spirit world keeping up with world events by tuning into television. I quickly jumped on that one with all sorts of images flashing through my mind. Now, lest you think that spirits loll around drinking beer and watching their favorite soap operas, or playing video games, let me point out that TV viewing, like most activities in the afterlife, has a purpose.

John revealed that spirits sometimes try to exert a subtle influence on our television coverage, particularly for important events: "When politicians are preparing and making their speeches, spirits are there, doing their best to help get the right message across." This positive influence has been made more difficult in recent years with the bitter hatred that has become evident in politics in many countries. Verbal abuse has become common, and recently physical assaults and all-in brawls have occurred in the heated debates of some parliaments.

Wondering whether my living room would sometimes be over-crowded with invisible viewers, I asked if spirits have to return to earth to watch TV. Do they have their own television sets in the afterlife, the ultimate smart TV? It turns out there is no technology required, as spirits are able to tune in directly by using what John described as "a thought process." This practice is also frequently used as a part of group learning in the afterlife, when the teacher wishes to emphasize a point using visual means, similar to what we on earth would see in a training session or seminar. John said the best way he can describe this ability is "very much like closing your eyes and picturing a television screen in your mind's eye, featuring a story from the last news program you watched." A spirit is able to project these images to others from their memory banks, either as a hologram or directly into their individual thoughts.

It sounds very much like science fiction, but, according to John, people on earth will be able to do the same in the not-too-distant future as part of other amazing mind creations. This will be part of the evolution of humans as we move out of the restrictions of three-dimensional reality into higher realms. There are already people on earth capable of these feats, and when the time is right they will pass on their knowledge to the rest of humanity.

54

Reincarnation

Reincarnation has always made sense to me, and even as a child I intuitively knew I had lived many lives before this one. I have a straightforward attitude to this subject. Why would we have only one chance at life as a human being in such a complex world? We live in a well-ordered universe subject to many cycles—planetary, seasonal, and organic—where life is far from random. It is not logical to my mind that some people can be born to affluence while millions exist in abject poverty. Is it just the luck of the draw that some people live a long and happy life while others die after a short or miserable existence? Is it just survival of the fittest? Dog eat dog?

I find it more logical that, as supposedly the highest developed life-forms on this planet, we are given more than one opportunity, enabling us to experience many aspects of life here. Otherwise, what is the purpose of it all? There is plenty of evidence for reincarnation, as I believe this book and my previous book—among others—document, and I do not intend to go into any further philosophical discussion here.

However, there are two questions I have been frequently asked during talks and in readings when the subject of reincarnation arises. Over to John and "Team Spirit" for the answers.

Firstly, with more than seven billion people on earth now, are spirits being recycled quicker than in past ages?

John's reply was short and to the point: "No, definitely not." Judy's earlier explanation (documented in chapter 38) of souls fragmenting in the afterlife to create new life provides a more comprehensive answer to this question.

The second question is, how long do we usually spend in the afterlife before reincarnating?

This will depend on our individual circumstances, with the understanding that there is no such thing as time in the world of spirit. When our guides and Elders consider us ready for another life, we will be offered the right opportunity. There are many threads to weave when life contracts are created by the Elders, involving the people and situations we will be working with in our next incarnation. There is no point in rushing back to another body if those people we most need to interact with are not going to be there at the same time. When you stop to think about it, our life contracts are so complicated, with so many potential directions and variables involved, the question of when and where we reincarnate is very complex. There are specialist spirits in the afterlife who put all these threads in place so that each life opportunity will not be wasted.

It is rather like organizing an international event like the Olympic Games and not giving it enough planning and preparation. When the opening ceremony gets under way, the host country may suddenly realize it has forgotten to officially invite a few key nations. It also may not have had enough time to build the swimming pavilion. Oops!

However, there are some spirits that do reincarnate quickly because they have an important role or purpose to fulfill. John refers to these people as "spiritual soldiers." Their job is to enter a body, carry out the required duties, leave, and then quickly reincarnate to continue their work.

Generally speaking, though, there is no rush for a spirit to reincarnate.

If life doesn't have that little bit of danger, you'd better create it. If life hands you that danger, accept it gratefully.

—SIR ANTHONY QUAYLE, 1913–1989,
British actor

55

Full Circle

As my exploration into the Heaven World drew to a close, my guide M contacted me in the dream state, suggesting that it would be most fitting to go full circle from where I started.

When I woke the next morning and remembered the dream, my mind automatically went back to the time spent with Ruth Phillips (née Wilson), who made the original connection with Judy in spirit a few months after she passed over in 1997. Ruth not only put the two of us back in contact again, but also told me I had been given permission by Spirit to develop my own abilities as a medium so that I could maintain contact with Judy. I had always been fascinated by the thought of communicating with people on the other side, and had occasionally enjoyed this by consulting other mediums. Even though

I had been working as a clairvoyant and astrologer, it did not mean I was also able to automatically communicate with people in the afterlife. Mediumship is a very special ability.

Uncovering this talent was slow work for me at first, but because I had a strong intention to communicate with Judy, I gradually started to open up to her and to the Heaven World. At first we were able to communicate quite well in group situations, as I now realize that I needed other people's energy to maintain contact. Judy would often "round up" spirits to be present in my spiritual development groups, and I soon dubbed her my "spirit wrangler." Eventually I learned how to achieve brief one-on-one communication with her, and Judy helped me open my mind to contact spirits when I was doing psychic consultations.

When I contacted Ruth, she was only too pleased to speak to Judy for me, even though they had not been in contact since 1997, and insisted that she would not read *Afterlife* beforehand. Ruth had read and approved only the chapter in which she was featured, and had no idea of the overall content of the book.

Before speaking with Ruth, I did a morning session of yoga and then contacted my guide M to check that the lines of communication were open and clear. M confirmed that Judy was ready and waiting, along with John and his team as backup, and he, too, would oversee it. I realized then the importance that was being placed on this connection.

Judy came through easily to Ruth, who described her as having "such a beautiful energy and with a big smile on her face." Ruth had met Judy only once, briefly, just before she passed over in 1997, so I am sure Judy's face was not etched on her mind. One of Judy's great features was a smile that lit up her whole face, but because she was exhausted and very close to passing when Ruth met her, that smile was rarely in evidence.

Judy's first message was that this is her "swan song," which made Ruth's presence so meaningful. Judy went on to say that this book completes the circle with her direct energy involved, and the next books that I write will be directed by what she termed "higher frequencies." Judy said her inspiration and mentorship are coming to a close and our contact will be less frequent from now on, as she is progressing to another level in the afterlife. This means that her soul vibration will be increasing to a higher frequency, making it harder for her to come back to communicate in earth's denser levels.

Judy says that the two books we worked on together were as much for her own development as mine, but now I will no longer have need for her input. I am well past the stage where I need proof of survival and I don't need to be in regular contact with her.

I had mixed feelings about this news: On one hand I was happy for Judy's soul to be advancing to new levels, while on the other I was sad at the thought of having much less contact with her.

Ruth was shown a vision of a lovely crystal orb symbolizing this completion phase, which she described as having a beautiful energy. Ruth experienced a sense of peace and love at this point, which she described as most gratifying.

Judy went on to give me some valuable advice about future books that I will be writing and encouragement for some other intriguing projects on the long road ahead, and informed me that there is still much work to do.

After Judy said her farewell, Ruth was told by her own guides that she and I had wandered in and out of each other's lives over many incarnations. Ruth was shown an image of us working together as fellow druids and bards in an ancient Celtic past life, one which she described as very meaningful.

Ah, but that is another story . . .

AFTERWORD

The wonderful thing writing about the afterlife and our past lives is that new information keeps pouring in. After completing this book, I received an intriguing message from Bob Murray in Canada. Bob is a highly respected medium and also the author of *The Stars Still Shine*, which chronicles the afterlife journey of his son-in-law Michael.

Bob is a regular guest on *Radio Out There* and in our off-air chats he often mentions that we have a strong past-life connection. Bob contacted me "out of the blue" to let me know about a very vivid past-life connection he had experienced, involving us both in the US Civil War.

When Bob sent me his story I was fascinated, as I have always known of a past life at this time, and have a long-standing interest in the Civil War. I have shared this information with only a couple of people, one of whom was my late partner, Judy, who was also a part of that life. Bob had no idea of this past life, let alone that I had fought with the Southern Confederate army, and was killed in a bloody battle.

Bob has kindly given permission to recount his story. . . .

The year was 1863 and two Englishmen, William Heath (now Robert Murray) and Reginald Cosgrove (now Barry Eaton) volunteered to go to the Confederate States of America on a buying trip. The mills of England needed raw cotton to continue production, but the American Civil War was raging. The Northern forces had created an embargo on the South, and British ships were not allowed in or out. William and Reginald were sent over to find a way around the blockade.

They first traveled to the West Indies, then by small coaster to some islands off the coast of North Carolina. From there they were smuggled to the mainland and Richmond, the capital of the Confederacy. Supplies in the way of war materiel were smuggled in, but nothing was going out. The two men soon realized that cotton was not being grown and existing stores were in critically short supply. Nothing was available for export, even if they could get through the blockade.

Both men were excellent horsemen and had served in a cavalry unit in England. They hadn't seen battle but were well trained. When they arrived, the decimated cavalry units were in the western part of the war zone, with very few remounts left. William and Reginald had limited choices: go back to England via the smugglers' route, or stay where they were. They decided to stay and volunteer their services to the Confederate army. After several months of inaction and frustration they both were given the honorary rank of colonel by General Robert E. Lee himself. He also swore them in as citizens of the Confederate States of America. It seems General Lee expected these new recruits to remain behind the lines and keep the many war widows comforted. They had other plans.

With the gold they had brought with them, they bought clothing, boots, hats, gloves, revolvers, long guns, and ammunition. They tore off any gold braid and any distinguishing bits of clothing that would identify them as officers or even soldiers. They kept their identity papers as British newspaper recorders (not reporters in those days). They gave their new citizenship papers to a bartender at the hotel where they were staying, swearing him to secrecy and ordering him to keep them safe.

In late June 1864 they took the supply train to Petersburg, Virginia. Once at the lines, the two men proved to be very useful. The third day at the front, William led a seven-man patrol behind enemy lines and managed to disrupt some Northern supply lines and create havoc when he torched a barn. He brought all his men back safely. Reginald, meanwhile, spoke with engineers about defensive positions and lines of fire. While William was leading the patrol, Reginald was organizing marksmen, or snipers, as they are called today. He wanted to lead night raiders but never got any volunteers.

William and Reginald slept in the trenches with the men as the Siege of Petersburg turned into trench warfare. Both were badly wounded on July 14, 1864, when a mortar shell landed in the trench.

However, they recovered from their wounds and went on for almost
another miserable year.

    On a spring day, April 2, 1865, at 8:15 in the morning, they were
killed.

I decided to do a little research of my own, and discovered that
the Third Battle of Petersburg started on April 2, 1865, and after a
ten-month siege the Confederate forces were finally defeated by a
superior force under General Ulysses S. Grant. A week later General
Robert E. Lee surrendered, and the war was virtually over.

Bob Murray received some further information a few weeks later,
when he connected with a powerful spirit in the Akashic Records section of the afterlife. The spirit, calling himself "Smith," spoke about
the importance of working with emotion when exploring past lives.
Bob provided me with a transcript of their contact:

> SMITH: Sometimes emotion is the way into the past life. In your
> time in Virginia during the Civil War, you and your friend Barry
> were filled with all kinds of emotion or you would have died old
> men back in England.

> BOB: Would you explain what you mean?

> SMITH: You went to the South to see if you could get cotton for
> the mills back in England. You wanted to break the blockade,
> but cotton was scarce. It was wartime and the Southerners just

weren't growing cotton. No cotton and no exports. You then had a choice.

BOB: Yes, we could go back to England or stay. We chose to stay.

SMITH: That was an emotional decision because you met some Southern belles.

BOB: And we stayed because of the women?

SMITH: Partly. Everybody tried to put on a noble front, a brave front, and there was plenty of emotion going around. You two were willing to sit out the war in the bars and taverns of Richmond but the two sisters you were "seeing" had a brother in Lee's army. He escaped from a Yankee prison and was brought back to Richmond, more dead than alive. When you first saw him, he was an emaciated skeleton with weeping sores and gaping wounds. He died shortly after he told you horror stories about the Yankees and what they did to prisoners.

BOB: So we up and enlisted for the Confederate cause?

SMITH: Not right then. You comforted the women but still didn't see the need to seek revenge for the loss of their brother. It was tragic, to be sure, but many others on both sides were being killed by the thousands. The South was losing men they couldn't replace, whereas the North was losing men but had replacements. It was a war of attrition, and the South was losing.

Lee knew that he couldn't win in any conventional way but wanted to influence the Northern public in such a way that they would get tired of the war and sue for peace or at least a stalemate. You two met General Lee and he changed your minds.

BOB: I think he give us citizenship and ranks in the Confederate army.

SMITH: It was honorary, but it impressed you. That part didn't change your mind, but what he told you did. Lee did not want his army to be in a siege. He knew that a mobile army couldn't be easily pinned down and could bring the fight to the enemy. He talked strategy with you because you and Barry were trained British cavalry officers. You agreed with his thinking and offered to help.

BOB: I don't think we helped all that much.

SMITH: Ah, but you did. You two saved many lives with your strategic tactics. Once the siege was laid, you and Barry used your engineering skills to build wicker willow baskets to contain the soil along the trenches. You both helped build tunnels, led raids, and kept supply lines going.

BOB: But we couldn't save the South.

SMITH: Of course not. Nobody could, not even in the early stages of the war. The industrial might of the North won over the agricultural South. Oh, at first the South seemed to be holding its own because of the inept handling of the Northern armies by politically appointed generals. When Sherman took over, it was the beginning of the end for the South.

BOB: No glory in getting ourselves blown up by a gigantic mortar shell.

SMITH: None whatsoever. By then you were very emotionally involved with your fellow soldiers. They were your comrades in arms. They laid down their lives for you and you did the same for them. To put it very mildly, all wars are a stupid waste of people and animals, but they do bring out the best of man in the worst of times. It also brings out the worst of man in the best of times.

BOB: So what did we learn, if anything? Are we better humans for that life? Are we more compassionate with our fellow humans?

SMITH: What do you think? I think you are, both of you.

NOTES

∽

1   Where to Explore Next?

   1. When spirit is used with a capital *S*, it denotes the collective energy of the spirit world, often referred to as "all that is."

4   The Puzzling Question of Time

   1. Sid Caesar quote from www.goodreads.com/author/quotes/142985.sid_caesar.

6   Challenges to Life Paths

   1. See www.drugabuse.gov/gsearch/genetic%2Binfluence.

7   The Dangers of Negativity

   1. John O'Donohue, *Anam Cara: A Book of Celtic Wisdom* (New York: HarperCollins Publishers, 1998).

11   Group Discussions in the Afterlife

   1. Helen Brown, *After Cleo Came Jonah* (Sydney: Allen & Unwin, 2012).

15   Meeting Kalingah

   1. Frank Joseph, ed., *The Lost Worlds of Ancient America* (Pompton Plains, NJ: New Page Books, 2012); reviewed in *Nexus Magazine* 14, no. 4 (June/July 2012).

17   The Wise Woman

1. Barbara Sher, *Wishcraft: How to Get What You Really Want* (New York: Ballantine Books, 1985).

20   The Wisdom of M

1. Silver Birch, spirit guide channeled by Maurice Barbanell, London medium and founder of *Psychic News*. From *The Silver Birch Book of Questions and Answers* (Oxshott, UK: Spiritual Truth Press, 1998).

35   Contacting Earth

1. Judith Chisholm, *Voices from Paradise* (Oxford: Jon Carpenter Publishing, 2000).

38   Information from the Akashic Records

1. Alice A. Bailey, *The Light of the Soul: Its Science and Effect: A Paraphrase of the Yoga Sutras of Patanjali* (New York: Lucis Publishing, 1927).

40   Judy's Funeral and Beyond

1. Michelle and Ezio De Angelis, *Postcards from the Other Side: True Stories of the Afterlife* (Sydney: Allen & Unwin, 2012).

41   Healing Past Wounds

1. See chapter 18 of my book *Afterlife: Uncovering the Secrets of Life After Death* (Sydney: Allen & Unwin, 2011).

46   Unconditional Love and Unresolved Emotions

1. Dr. Stephanie Sarkis, "Here, There, and Everywhere: 30 Quotes on Forgiveness," *Psychology Today*, February 11, 2011, http://www .psychologytoday.com/blog/here-there-and-everywhere/201102 /30-quotes-forgiveness.

48   Accidents, Suicide, Euthanasia, and Comas

1. Larry King special, *Dinner with the Kings*, CNN, December 4, 2011, www.cryogenicsociety.org/16669/news/Larry_King_I_Wanna_Be _Frozen.
2. See Wikipedia's List of Agnostics, http://en.wikipedia.org/wiki/List_of _agnostics.

49 Mental Health Conditions

1. Ray Moynihan and Alan Cassels, *Selling Sickness: How Drug Companies Are Turning Us All into Patients* (Sydney: Allen & Unwin, 2005), 198.
2. Craig Hamilton with Will Swanton, *A Better Life: How Our Darkest Moments Can Be Our Greatest Gift* (Sydney: Allen & Unwin, 2012).

FURTHER READING

Chisholm, Judith. *Voices from Paradise*. Oxford, UK: Jon Carpenter Publishing, 2000.

De Angelis, Michelle, and Ezio De Angelis. *Postcards from the Other Side: True Stories of the Afterlife*. Sydney: Allen & Unwin, 2012.

DuBois, Allison. *Talk to Me: What the Dead Whisper in Your Ear*. Sydney: Allen & Unwin, 2012.

Eaton, Barry. *Afterlife: Uncovering the Secrets of Life After Death*. Sydney: Allen & Unwin, 2011.

Linn, Denise. *Past Lives, Present Dreams: How to Use Reincarnation for Personal Growth*. London: Piatkus, 1994.

Moynihan, Ray. *Sex, Lies and Pharmaceuticals: How Drug Companies Are Bankrolling the Next Big Condition for Women*. Sydney: Allen & Unwin, 2010.

Moynihan, Ray, and Alan Cassels: *Selling Sickness: How Drug Companies Are Turning Us All into Patients*. Sydney: Allen & Unwin, 2005.

Ramster, Peter. *The Search for Lives Past*. Somerset Film & Publishing, 1990.

Stoller, Galen. *My Life After Life: A Posthumous Memoir*. Lagunitas, CA: Dream Treader Press, 2011.

Tymn, Michael. *Transcending the Titanic: Beyond Death's Door*. Guildford, UK: White Crow Books, 2012.

Weiss, Brian L., MD. *Many Lives, Many Masters*. New York: Simon & Schuster, 1988.

Zammit, Victor, and Wendy Zammit. *A Lawyer Presents the Evidence for the Afterlife: Irrefutable Objective Evidence*. Guildford, UK: White Crow Books, 2013.

ABOUT THE AUTHOR

——————— ∽ ———————

For most of his professional life, Barry Eaton has been a radio and television presenter, MC, producer, and writer.

His first book, *Afterlife: Uncovering the Secrets of Life After Death*, was published by Allen & Unwin in 2011 and has been released internationally to wide acclaim.

ABC television viewers in Australia with long memories may recall him as the face of the weekly show *Sportsview*, and the host of such events as the Bicentennial telecast, the New Zealand Commonwealth Games, and the ABC news. He also hosted many entertainment specials, interviewed a galaxy of stars, and has even had a stint as a weather forecaster. These days he prefers giving astrological forecasts.

In a long and varied career, Barry has also worked as a presenter, talk-show host, and commentator in commercial radio and television; hosted and produced his own in-house tourism television show; run a media consultancy; and produced television documentaries. He is widely heard through his voice-over work on radio and television and internationally for wildlife documentaries on cable TV.

Barry originally trained as an actor, and has appeared on film and television and in several stage productions. He narrated two Military Tattoo Arena Spectaculars in 2006 and 2008, describing them as "the most satisfying shows I have worked on."

With his personal life in turmoil in 1990, Barry's spiritual journey took a new turn. He sought answers first through the study of astrology and then other areas such as psychic research, reincarnation, numerology, mediumship, metaphysics, spiritual healing, and much more.

Since then he has consulted, written, and lectured on many holistic subjects, as well as continuing his own research. Barry currently hosts *Radio Out There*, a popular Internet program that delves into the mysteries of the universe. Hosting and producing these shows provide an opportunity to work with and interview a huge number of healers, psychics, mediums, alternative practitioners, authors, and fellow travelers in the metaphysical world. He also works as an intuitive reader/medium.

A lecturer in radio journalism at Macleay College in Sydney from 1995 to 1999, Barry then became faculty coordinator of journalism. He wrote an astrology page for the magazine *For Me* in 1998, as well as freelance columns and articles for various alternative magazines. He has also written many travel and entertainment features, which have been widely published.